Extraordinary Jobs in

LEISURE

Also in the Extraordinary Jobs series:

Extraordinary Jobs in

LEISURE

ALECIA T. DEVANTIER & CAROL A. TURKINGTON

Ferguson
An imprint of Infobase Publishing

Extraordinary Jobs in Leisure

Copyright © 2007 by Alecia T. Devantier and Carol A. Turkington

Ferguson
An imprint of Infobase Publishing, Inc.
132 West 31st Street
New York NY 10001

Library of Congress Cataloging-in-Publication Data
Devantier, Alecia T.
  Extraordinary jobs in Leisure / Alecia T. Devantier and Carol A. Turkington.
    p. cm.—(Extraordinary jobs)
  Includes bibliographical references and index.
  ISBN 0-8160-5859-8 (hc: alk. paper)
1. Recreation—Vocational guidance. 2. Leisure—Vocational guidance. I. Turkington, Carol. II. Title. III. Series: Devantier, Alecia T. Extraordinary Jobs series.
  GV160.D48 2006
  790.023—dc 22   2006011388

Ferguson books are available at special discounts when purchased in bulk quantities for businesses, associations, institutions, or sales promotions. Please call our Special Sales Department in New York at (212) 967-8800 or (800) 322-8755.

You can find Ferguson on the World Wide Web at http://www.fergpubco.com

Text design by Mary Susan Ryan-Flynn
Cover design by Salvatore Luongo

Printed in the United States of America

VB MSRF 10 9 8 7 6 5 4 3 2 1

This book is printed on acid-free paper.

CONTENTS

ACKNOWLEDGMENTS

This book wouldn't have been possible without the help of countless others who referred us to individuals to interview and came up with information about a wide variety of odd and unusual jobs. We deeply appreciate the time and generosity of all those individuals who took the time to talk to us about their unusual jobs in the world of leisure. Thanks also to all the people who helped with interviews and information and the production of this book, including Jon Rand and Susan Shelly McGovern. Thanks also to our editors James Chambers and Sarah Fogarty, to Vanessa Nittoli, to our agents Ed Claflin of Ed Claflin Literary Associates and Gene Brissie of James Peter Associates, and to Michael and Kara.

ARE YOU CUT OUT FOR A CAREER IN LEISURE?

Your files are piled so high on your desk that you can't find your coffee mug. You're due to give a big presentation in front of the board in 10 minutes, and you can't remember for the life of you what you'd planned to say. You've spent so much time on the job you might as well just sleep in your cubicle.

This doesn't appeal to you?

If you can't stand the thought of sitting at a desk every day, gazing out your window at the world passing you by, then maybe you should consider a career in the leisure industry, doing what you love to do—planning sci-fi conventions, working on a cruise ship or Club Med Island, whatever—rather than what you feel obligated to do. Let's face it: Some people just aren't cut out for a typical career path carved out for them by others. But how do you know if you're more the ski lift–operating, magic-filled, trapeze artist kind of person? Take some time to think about the kind of person you are and the sorts of experiences you dream of having.

First of all, ask yourself: What am I passionate about? Do you spend every waking moment thinking and dreaming about being shot out of a cannon? Do you watch the circus on TV and yearn to strut around the center ring in a top hat and tails? Did you fall so in love with skydiving that you dream of someday teaching other students the same thing? Do you love the idea of working at a resort, vacation destination, theme park, or cruise ship? Does the idea of helping other people have fun seem like the very best kind of job there is?

If you follow your heart, you're almost guaranteed to find a career you will love. In fact, almost every individual we interviewed for this book repeated the same litany—*I love my job. I love the independence.*

Sadly, jobs in the leisure industry often don't pay very much—with a few exceptions. Yet while most of these careers don't offer monetary rewards, to the people who pursue those careers, it doesn't seem to matter. What these jobs do offer is something much harder to measure—and that's a job that lets your spirit soar, that allows you to do what you love to do.

You can't put a price on that.

Of course, loving what you do is only part of having a successful career in the leisure industry. You've also got to be good at what you want to do. Most leisure jobs are so specialized that if you're going to go after one of them, you need to be really good at it. Whether you're thinking of becoming a skydiver or an auctioneer, you need to have the talent and the training to do that job better than most other people.

If you're like most of us, you've inherited a bevy of *shoulds* about the kind of person you are. These *shoulds* inside your head can be a major stumbling block in finding and enjoying a leisure career. Maybe other people won't be so happy with your career choice either. You may hear complaints from your family and friends who just can't understand why you don't want a "regular job." If you confide your career dreams to some of these people, they may try to discourage you. Can you handle their continuous skepticism, or downright disappointment? Other people often have their own *shoulds* for you too.

Or maybe you're having a hard time imagining a different path for yourself because of the obstacles you see. Maybe you're saying to yourself: "There's just no way I can follow my dream and make a living. I don't have the right education," or "I don't have the right background," or "I'm the wrong gender," or "I'm the wrong color." Tyron McFarlan, who you'll read about in this book, is one of only two African-American ringmasters ever hired by Ringling Bros. and Barnum & Bailey in 134 years. But he didn't give up on his dream, and neither should you. He's successful because he wouldn't accept someone else's assessment that he couldn't do what he loved to do because of the color of his skin.

If you get bogged down in the belief that you can't follow your dream because of what is, you take away your power to discover what could be. You lose the power to create a different future.

A few of the people we've talked to in this book have always known exactly what they wanted to do, and did it. But almost everyone else ended up with a job in the leisure industry by a circuitous route. It can take years to work up the courage to actually do what we knew all along we would have loved to do. You'll find that going after a job in the leisure industry is usually built slowly out of a variety of different experiences.

You don't have to start big. Try unique educational experiences—take a skydiving class. Try an internship or unconventional job, a summer job, travel, or volunteer work.

Try not to think of learning and working as two totally separate things. When somebody hands you a diploma, you don't stop learning. School can be the best place to build up your fact-based knowledge; the rest of your life provides you with experience-based knowledge. You need both of those types of knowledge to forge a career in the leisure industry. Remember that this type of career is usually an active experience—take charge of your journey instead of relying on someone else's career path. Take advantage of the things you learn as you plan your next experience.

If you do decide to seek out a career in the leisure industry, you'll almost certainly encounter setbacks. How do you handle adversity? How do you feel when you fail? If you've always wanted to be a running coach, how are you going to feel if you can't seem to break into the business, or no one wants to hire you? If you can pick yourself up and keep going, you've probably got the temperament to survive.

Going after the career you want means you'll need to look at the world through curious eyes—to wonder what's on the other side of the mountain and actually go there to find out. By exploring your options, you'll learn that work and play become the same thing. Push past your doubts and fears—and let your journey begin!

Carol A. Turkington
Alecia T. Devantier

HOW TO USE THIS BOOK

Students face a lot of pressure to decide what they want to be when they grow up. For some students, the decision is easy, but for others, it's a real struggle. If you're not interested in a traditional 9-to-5 job and you're eyeing the field of leisure pursuits as a unique way to make a living, where can you go to find out about these exciting, nontraditional jobs?

For example, where can you go to find out how to become an auctioneer, gaveling down antiques? What does it take to become a sci-fi convention planner, mapping out exciting experiences for fans? Where do you learn how to be a theme park manager? Is it really possible to make a living as an aerialist? Where would you go for training if you wanted to be a human cannonball or a golf course superintendent? What's the job outlook for limo drivers?

Look no further! This book will take you inside the world of a number of different jobs in the leisure field, answering questions you might have, letting you know what to expect if you pursue that career, introducing you to someone making a living that way, and providing resources if you want to do further research.

THE JOB PROFILES

All job profiles in this book have been broken down into the following fact-filled sections: At a Glance, Overview, and Interview. Each offers a distinct perspective on the job, and taken together give you a full view of the job in question.

At a Glance

Each entry starts out with an "At a Glance" box, offering a snapshot of important basic information to give you a quick glimpse of that particular job, including salary, education, experience, personal attributes, requirements, and outlook.

✔ *Salary range.* What can you expect to make? Salary ranges for the jobs in this book are as accurate as possible; many are based on the U.S. Bureau of Labor Statistics' *Occupational Outlook Handbook*. Information also comes from individuals, actual job ads, employers, and experts in that field. It's important to remember that salaries for any particular job vary greatly depending on experience, geographic location, and level of education.

✔ *Education/Experience.* What kind of education or experience does the job require? This section will give you some information about the types of education or experience requirements the job might call for.

✔ *Personal attributes.* Do you have what it takes to do this job? How do you think of yourself? How would someone else describe you? This section will give you an idea of some of the personality characteristics and traits that might be useful to you if you choose this career. These attributes were collected from articles written about the job, as well as recommendations from employers and people actually doing the jobs, working in the field.

☑ *Requirements.* Are you qualified? You might as well make sure you meet any health, medical, or screening requirements before going any further with your job pursuit.

☑ *Outlook.* What are your chances of finding a job in the leisure industry? This section is based in part on the *Occupational Outlook Handbook*, as well as on interviews with employers and experts. This information is typically a "best guess" based on the information that's available right now, including changes in the economy, situations in United States and around the world, job trends, and retirement levels. These and many other factors can influence changes in the availability of jobs in the leisure industry.

Overview

This section will give you an idea of what to expect from the job. For most of these unusual jobs, there really is no such thing as an average day. Each day is a whole new adventure, bringing with it a unique set of challenges and rewards. This section will give you an idea of what a person in this position might expect on a day-to-day basis.

The overview also gives you more details about how to get into the profession, offering a more detailed look at the required training or education, if needed, and providing an in-depth look at what to expect during that training or educational period.

No job is perfect, and **Pitfalls** takes a look at some of the obvious and maybe not-so-obvious pitfalls of the job. Don't let the pitfalls discourage you from pursuing a career; they are just things to be aware of while making your decision.

For many people, loving their job so much that they look forward to going to work every day is enough of a perk. **Perks** looks at some of the other perks of the job you may not have considered.

What can you do now to start working toward the career of your dreams? **Get a Jump on the Job** will give you some ideas and suggestions for things that you can do now, even before graduating, to start preparing for this job. Opportunities include training programs, internships, groups and organizations to join, as well as practical skills to learn.

Interview

In addition to taking a general look at the job, each entry features a discussion with someone who is lucky enough to do this job for a living. In addition to giving you an inside look at the job, this interview provides valuable tips for anyone interested in pursuing a career in the same field.

APPENDIXES

Appendix A (Associations, Organizations, and Web Sites) lists of places to look for additional information about each specific job, including professional associations, societies, unions, government organizations, training programs, forums, official government links, and periodicals. Associations and other groups are a great source of information, and there's an association for just about every job you can imagine. Many groups and associations have a student membership level, which you can join by paying a small fee. There are many advantages to joining an association, including the chance to make important contacts, receive helpful newsletters, and attend workshops or conferences. Some associations also offer scholarships that will make it easier to further your education.

In **Appendix B (Online Career Resources)** we've gathered some of the best general Web sites about unusual jobs in the leisure industry, along with a host of very specific Web sites tailored to individual leisure jobs. Use these as a springboard to your own Internet research. Of course, all of this information was current as this book was written, but Web site addresses do change. If you can't find what you're looking for at a given address, do a simple Internet search—the page may have been moved to a different location.

READ MORE ABOUT IT

In this back-of-the-book listing, we've gathered some helpful books that can give you more detailed information about each job we discuss in this book. Find these at the library or bookstore if you want to learn even more about leisure jobs.

AERIALIST

OVERVIEW

You've probably heard the lyrics: *He floats through the air with the greatest of ease, this daring young man on the flying trapeze.* Of all the circus acts that capture the imagination, there's none more daring and dangerous. An aerialist is any circus artist who performs acrobatic feats in the air, and that includes those daredevils on the high wire. But the best-known aerialists are the trapeze artists, who take our breath away by swinging through the air on a bar, performing flips in midair, and getting caught by a partner who's hanging upside down from another bar. The top trapeze artists perform without safety devices. They can earn excellent incomes because few other people can do what they do. Most aerialists, including trapeze artists, are born into circus families and learn their skills from their parents. But several clubs and schools also teach trapeze skills.

Beginners start on the ground with a practice bar. You'll learn how to swing while sitting on the bar and then while hanging upside down by your knees. When you've learned these techniques, you'll climb to a small platform 30 feet in the air. You're not supposed to look down but if you do, you'll be grateful to have a net below and a safety harness around your waist that's connected to a safety line. You'll lean from the platform and grab the bar with both hands. Your first leap of faith will come when you swing towards a bar on the other side of the arena while you're hanging by your knees. If you haven't had a heart attack yet, you'll catch the other bar, then somersault into the net.

Once you get the hang of this, you might try swinging into the hands of a catcher, who hangs by the knees from the catch bar. That person will catch you by your wrists and swing you before allowing you to drop to the net. And this is just a basic routine. Imagine flying through the air while doing flips, like an Olympic diver going off the high board. Then imagine trying this without safety equipment, and the catcher being all that stands between you and the arena floor. Of course, you'll perfect this routine with the aid of safety equipment before you try it without a net.

Sylvia Zerbini, aerialist and equestrienne

Sylvia Zerbini grew up in the circus. Her father, Tarzan, was an eighth-generation performer from an Italian circus family, and her mother, Jacqueline, was a second-generation performer from a French circus family. With a mother who was a trapeze artist and a father who trained animals, Zerbini combined both specialties for one of the most unusual acts in the Ringling Bros. and Barnum & Bailey Circus.

In her act, Zerbini sends eight beautiful horses, running free, into the arena. Zerbini then gallops into the ring on a horse, grabs a trapeze bar and hoists herself 40 feet, swings down, drops to the ground, and performs a nine-minute aerial and horse show. She owns, trains, and transports the horses herself.

Zerbini was only five years old when she first performed in front of an audience. "I was sitting on top of an elephant!" she recalls. "And no, I can't really say I was scared. My family has been circus performers for nine generations, so it pretty much came natural to me."

Zerbini performed her first aerial routine when she was eight years old and playing on her mother's backyard trapeze. One day, all alone, she imitated her mother doing a half-body twist before catching the bar with her heels. "I told my parents, 'I can do that. Want to see?'" Zerbini says. "My mom and dad came over and I did it. They thought, 'Oh, my God!'"

By the time she was 12, Zerbini was working on the trapeze. "When you're young, of course, you don't realize what you're doing," she says. "I was 20 feet in the air, and fear of falling never entered my mind. As you get older, you start to pay attention." At the age of 25, Zerbini had a daughter and began to worry what would happen if she got hurt. "In trapeze, you can't do that because then I'd second guess my movements," she says. "An hour before a performance, I don't talk to anybody. You just totally learn how to block everything out, listen to music and stretch."

A lack of fear is crucial to the success of trapeze artists. Those who grow up in a circus family often practice dangerous routines before they're old enough to know they're supposed to be scared. They're like kids put on horseback before they are old enough to seriously consider the perils of getting thrown. But while trapeze artists may be immune to fear, they're not immune to injury. Some quit because their shoulders become chronically sore or they tire of constant blisters and bruises on their heels and hands.

By now, you're probably starting to understand the tremendous dedication and discipline needed to become a trapeze artist. You'll often perform two or three shows a day, even if you're tired, injured, or ill. And you'll still take time to practice and work out because the job requires you to stay slim and strong. You'll travel each week from one city to another with just one full day off. Most performers get periodic breaks during the year, yet their job is still a grind. And they still have to pay bills, do laundry, and perhaps tend to family matters. Circus performers often travel with their spouses and children.

The Flying Wallendas are the most famous aerialists and circus family of all time. They had a traveling European circus as far back as 1780 and later became famous for their daring on the flying trapeze and high wire. Led by patriarch Karl Wallenda, the family developed an amazing four-person,

Zerbini experienced her worst accident in 2000, when her heel failed to catch the bar and she fell 30 feet headfirst and landed on her shoulder. "I tore everything in my shoulder," she says. "They told me that if I didn't have so many muscles, I probably would've snapped my bone in half. With therapy, they told me I'd be out at least six months. Three months later, I was performing again." During one practice mishap, in which she was 45 feet in the air, Zerbini escaped with a twisted ankle and bruises that kept her out less than a week.

Accidents don't frighten Zerbini—they make her angry. "I get mad," she says, "because I've been doing this for so long and done everything imaginable that you can do in the air. So when I do something that's not 100 percent right and I fall, I totally don't accept it. My madness overcomes my fear. Every time something goes wrong, it's my fault. I'm not paying attention. The mechanics of movement should always be the same."

To Zerbini, discipline is the most important thing. "I'm working in a bodysuit that's super tight, like a catsuit," she says. "I cannot have an ounce of fat. I hang by my toes and knees, so I can't take baths in performance weeks. Your skin gets soft and you can't let it get slippery." Performing night after night can take its toll. "If I have a muscle pull or a fever, you have to go out in front of thousands of people, so what can you do?" she says. "But I still get through the routine. Your mind is the strongest muscle in the whole body."

Zerbini's daughter, Ambra, is the tenth generation of this circus family. When she was 12, she was performing in a barnyard routine with pigs, goats, and a pony, and rode one of her mother's stallions in the circus parade. Zerbini didn't object if her daughter wanted to follow in her footsteps, but she wasn't going to push her. "As a young girl, I knew exactly what I wanted to do," she says. "My daughter's undecided. She loves the horses but sometimes she says, 'I want to play soccer…I want to be a cheerleader.'"

three-level pyramid on the high wire. Karl Wallenda balanced on a chair on top of a bar between the shoulders of two men on bicycles. Karl's wife, Helen, stood on his shoulders. The Wallendas came to the United States in 1928 and were an immediate sensation. Their act evolved into a seven-person pyramid, and a 1962 accident in Detroit resulted in the death of two performers and the paralysis of a third. Karl Wallenda fell to his death in 1978 at age 73 because of faulty equipment. The family still performs in separate acts but has reunited for special appearances. In 2001, the Wallendas assembled an unprecedented eight-person, three-level pyramid. To further cement their place in aerial history, they added two more Wallendas to form the first ever 10-person pyramid. As the old warning goes—*don't try this at home*.

Pitfalls

You can expect to suffer strains, bruises, and even serious falls. Trapeze artists and other aerialists may work six days a week and spend most of the year on the road. It's a challenge to keep your personal life in order while you're with the circus. Wages often are low at the smaller circuses until you work your way up to the big time and a six-figure income.

Perks

The pay can be excellent if you're at the top of your profession. Circus performers often enjoy a show's camaraderie. They also enjoy the same exhilaration and popularity as most top-notch entertainers.

Get a Jump on the Job

If you're not born into a circus family, you can attend a school or join a club in which young people learn circus skills. You can find the club nearest you through the American Youth Circus Organization Web site, http://www.americanyouthcircus.org. A trip to the circus will give you a good idea of whether you'd like to be up on the trapeze or high wire or are just content to watch.

AUCTIONEER

OVERVIEW

When most of us shop for furniture, appliances, clothes, or baseball gloves, we check the price tag and know exactly how much to pay. But some goods and properties are sold through auctions, in which buyers bid against each other and the highest bidder wins. At an auction, you can buy livestock, large quantities of fruits and vegetables, real estate, cars, antiques, artwork, and much more.

Auctioneers are best known for their rhythmic chant: "A hundred, do I have a hundred fifty? A hundred fifty, do I have two hundred? Two hundred going once . . . two hundred going twice . . . sold." And down comes the hammer to signal that the $200 bid has been accepted.

Auctioning has been going on for thousands of years—all the way back to ancient Greece, around 500 B.C. Auctions later became popular in England, where two of the world's most famous auction houses have operated for more than two centuries: Sotheby's, founded in 1744, and Christie's, in 1766.

An auctioneer works for the sellers and is paid a commission (a fixed percentage of sales) or a flat fee. Although an auctioneer's work is showcased on auction day, it actually starts long before the opening bid. First, the auctioneer must organize the merchandise and research its value. He or she inspects the items to make sure they're suitable, lists them in a catalog, and sets up a display for the merchandise to be inspected by potential bidders. The auctioneer must also be aware of business or legal issues. If items are being auctioned to help a bankrupt person or company pay

AT A GLANCE

Salary Range
$30,000 to $100,000+

Education/Experience
You can learn the basics at auction school. You'll also have to know a lot about the value and quality of the goods or property you'll be selling. If you want to be a real estate auctioneer, for instance, it would help to have experience as a real estate broker.

Personal Attributes
You need self-confidence to assure buyers that they're bidding on worthwhile merchandise. You'll have to be comfortable addressing large groups of people and be able to work quickly and under pressure.

Requirements
You'll need a strong, clear voice that can work for hours. Some auctioneers boost their credentials by becoming certified personal property appraisers.

Outlook
As long as Americans love auctions, there will be plenty of auctioneers, even with online auctions competing for their business. But the most glamorous and highest-paying auctions are often run by a small number of professionals who may keep their jobs for decades.

off debt, the auctioneer must get approval from the creditors. The auctioneer places advertising to attract a big crowd.

At auctions involving very expensive items, sellers may let their merchandise go only for a minimum bid. This is called a *reserve price*, which is set before the auction. At most auctions, however, the high bidder wins, no matter the price.

Once an auctioneer has completed preparations, it's time to step up to the microphone and let the auction begin. The

Walt Robertson, thoroughbred auctioneer

Auctions don't get much more glamorous than those involving thoroughbred racehorses. Auctioneers wear tuxedoes and start their patter as well-bred horses are led into the sales ring before an audience filled with oil sheiks, business tycoons, movie stars, and top horse trainers. If James Bond hadn't liked casinos so much, he could just as easily have found high-stakes bidding and a jet-set crowd at a thoroughbred auction. Bidders pay millions for yearlings that grow up to run—and perhaps win—important races. Sometimes a lucky bidder gets a future Kentucky Derby winner at a bargain basement price.

Walt Robertson is president of Fasig-Tipton, a thoroughbred sales company based in Lexington, Kentucky, in the heart of horse country. He's also one of four auctioneers who conduct the company's 15 to 20 sales a year. At a 2005 auction in Florida for two-year-olds in training, 147 horses were sold for $50 million. Fasig-Tipton charges a 5 percent commission on sales plus a small entry fee for each horse. So many horses are nominated for Fasig-Tipton's biggest sales that Robertson can't accommodate all the breeders. For just three yearling sales in a year, Fasig-Tipton will get about 3,500 applications but accept only about 1,000. Robertson and his colleagues try to pick the best horses for their catalog. Thoroughbred sellers routinely set a reserve price for their horses, often with Robertson's advice.

"We will screen these horses on pedigree," Robertson says. "The ones that are suitable, we will make a physical inspection and spend the months of March and April looking at horses all over the United States. We're looking at conformation and try to pick the most athletic-looking horses. There are six of us who do it, and we go out in pairs." A horse with a good pedigree comes from a family that's produced winners of big races. Breeders like to say that they breed the best to the best and hope for the best. A horse's conformation is its physical structure. Kentucky Derby–winning trainer D. Wayne Lukas, who often bids millions of dollars for his clients, has had exceptional success with yearling fillies bought at auctions. He says he looks for the head of a princess, the rear end of a washerwoman, and the walk of a movie star.

"Any auctioneer, whether he handles real estate, wine, art, or furniture, needs to have a pretty good knowledge of his product and needs of his customers," Robertson says. "You need to have a pretty good knowledge of the people you're selling to. When you do that, you get respect. Just like in any other profession, the guy who works hardest wins." Being able to evaluate a horse's pedigree and conformation takes years of study and experience. Robertson learned about horses from his

auctioneer will introduce the auction staff, then explain the reason for the sale and order in which the items will be sold. The auctioneer will also explain the rules of the sale, the deadline for buyers to claim their items, whether any items are under warranty, and if buyers can pay by cash, check, or credit card. The auctioneer may also answer any questions from potential bidders.

The auctioneer will then start presenting items. Because he or she is trying to get the best possible price, the auctioneer likes to make a sales pitch to explain why an item is valuable or attractive. The auctioneer will set a starting price and ask for the first bid, then for higher bids until the bidding stops. A good auctioneer keeps the price rising without asking for a bid that's so high that it kills the bidding. Bidders father, Jim, a Kentuckian who bought, sold, and trained show horses. The elder Robertson would hire an auctioneer for his sales and Walt and his brother were enlisted to help. Walt became an auctioneer after graduating from the University of Kentucky and attending auction school in Mason City, Iowa. "They get you over your stage fright and get you into a rhythm," he says.

Now Robertson is the auctioneer at some of the world's biggest horse sales in Miami, Saratoga Springs (N.Y.), and Lexington. First, an announcer introduces the horse being led into the ring and describes its pedigree. Then Robertson, aided by several spotters around the audience, starts the bidding. "You try to use your voice right," he says. "Like a singer, you try to work from pretty deep inside your throat and push with your diaphragm to make your voice last longer. You can get pretty tired and if you get a cold, you're going to be hoarse, no matter what you do."

Although a sale may include hundreds of horses, the auction of just one important horse can become an event in itself. Just three months after Smarty Jones won the 2004 Kentucky Derby, his mother, I'll Get Along, was auctioned by Fasig-Tipton. She was pregnant by Smarty Jones's father, Elusive Quality, which raised hopes for another Derby winner. She was sold for $5 million. "You remember the big ones, of course you do," Robertson says. "When you sell a mare that important, it's pretty special. There'll always be a big crowd there to see it happen because of the buildup and the hype. Thank God she sold well and was deserving of every bit of hype she had. There's electricity up and down the line. I try to get as pumped up as my buyers and sellers."

Many thoroughbred owners let their trainers or bloodstock agents bid for them. Some bidders are so publicity-shy that only a trained eye can tell that they're bidding. "The buyers who want to remain anonymous will usually set something up with the auctioneer or spotter," Robertson says. "Maybe they'll have a prearranged signal, and you know to watch them. If D. Wayne Lukas is in the room, you keep an eye on him. You won't miss those fellas very often. And the ones who would like anonymity, we know who they are."

Although the biggest buyers and sellers get the most attention and generate the biggest commissions, Robertson tries to make sure the smaller buyers and sellers don't get overlooked. "It's terrific to sell a big horse, but the next horse in the ring is also important, especially to the next seller," he says. "Until we sell his horse and he gets what he needs, that's the important thing. We cannot lose sight of that."

will raise their hands or make other signals. At large auctions, spotters help make sure that no bidders get overlooked.

You can break into this business by attending an auction school. The Missouri Auction School, the nation's best-known school of its kind, teaches students to develop their own chant and arranges for them to practice at live auctions. Students learn the business skills needed to conduct auctions. They also attend workshops that specialize in antiques, autos, real estate, and other items that are popular at auctions.

Pitfalls

Auctioneers spend a lot of time traveling to inspect merchandise or meet with sellers. During auctions, their legs and voices can become very tired, and they routinely work long hours, including evenings and weekends.

Perks

You can work as long as your voice, health, and enthusiasm hold up. For many auctioneers, their work is an extension of their hobbies, such as collecting antiques, stamps, or cars. Most auctioneers love their work because they're not tied down to a desk and they deal with a wide variety of merchandise and people. Pay can be excellent for those who stay busy and deal with valuable merchandise. Many auctioneers work part time for extra income or with the aim of getting enough business to go full time.

Get a Jump on the Job

Learn as much as you can about the kinds of items that are sold at auctions. Attend local auctions and observe the auctioneer's techniques. You even might try making a bid. Instead of holding a yard sale to clear out your room, conduct an auction.

CASINO DEALER

OVERVIEW

The casino dealer is the one with the glamorous job, dealing out cards and running games of chance at flashy casinos, entertaining guests by operating a gaming table according to specific rules. While casino gaming has been legal in Nevada for more than seven decades and in Atlantic City, N.J., for more than 25 years, it wasn't until the late 1980s and early 1990s that other places across the country began to introduce commercial casino gaming. Today, commercial casinos are located in 11 states and many tribal lands, bringing lots of benefits to the host states and local communities.

Dealers operate table games such as craps, blackjack, and roulette. You'll find them standing or sitting behind the table, providing dice, dealing cards, and running the equipment. Dealers also keep a close watch over the patrons looking for infractions of casino rules. But that's not all; dealers also determine winners, calculate and pay winning bets, and collect losing bets. Because of the fast-paced work environment, most gaming dealers must be competent in at least two games (usually blackjack and craps). The more games you can deal, the more valuable you'll be to the casino (especially during the graveyard shift, when the volume of business can be hard to predict). Some casinos may have different levels of casino dealers, depending on the variety of games dealt.

The atmosphere can get tense when a customer is playing for big stakes, and dealers must be very careful not to make

AT A GLANCE

Salary Range

Wage earnings for dealers vary according to level of experience, training, location, and size of the gaming establishment. Average earnings for dealers are $14,090, ranging from $12,000 to $20,820, but tips make the salary much higher.

Education/Experience

No common minimum educational requirements; each casino establishes its own requirements for education, training, and experience. Some gaming occupations demand special skills, such as dealing blackjack, which are unique to casino work. Most employers prefer a high school diploma or GED. Almost all provide some in-house training in addition to requiring certification. The type and quantity of classes needed may vary. Many institutions of higher learning give training toward certification in gaming, as well as offering an associate's, bachelor's, or master's degree in a hospitality-related field such as hospitality management, hospitality administration, or hotel management. Some schools offer training in games, gaming supervision, slot attendant and slot repair technician work, slot department management, and surveillance and security.

Personal Attributes

Casino gaming workers provide entertainment and hospitality to patrons, and how good they are at their jobs affects a casino's success or failure. Gaming workers need good communication skills, an outgoing personality, and the ability to maintain their composure even when dealing with angry or demanding patrons. Personal integrity is also important, because workers handle large amounts of money.

Requirements

Nearly all gaming dealers are certified. Certification is available through two- or four-year programs in gaming or a hospitality-related field. Workers need a license issued by a regulatory agency, such as a

(continues)

AT A GLANCE (continued)

state casino control board or commission. Applicants for a license must provide photo identification, offer proof of residency in the state in which they anticipate working, and pay a fee, plus submit to a background check. Age requirements vary by state. Gaming dealers must be skilled in customer service and in executing their game.

Outlook

You'll have the best chance for a job if you have a degree or certification in gaming or a hospitality-related field, previous training or experience in casino gaming, and the ability to get along with people. Because experienced dealers can attract new and repeat customers, they usually have the best chance at landing a job. As the popularity of gaming continues to increase, employment in gaming services occupations is expected to grow faster than the average for all occupations through 2012. As more states realize the financial windfall from casinos, they are overlooking their previous opposition to legalized gambling and will probably approve building more casinos through the early 2000s. Because of the demand for more table games in casinos, rapid growth is expected among dealers.

As the population grows and is willing to spend more money, the popularity of gaming also increases. As competition for gaming patrons grows, there should be more jobs available for dealers. Most jobs may occur in established gaming areas such as Las Vegas and Atlantic City, as well as in other states and areas that may legalize gaming in the coming years, including casinos on Indian tribal lands.

any mistakes. Because of the high pressure of handling large amounts of money, game dealers typically get a break every hour.

A good dealer will try to be friendly so players will feel like they're having a good time even when they lose—because it's

the player who forks over the tip. Players having fun and enjoying themselves are more likely to leave a tip even after a bad session. Some players give a dealer a tip by making a bet for them as they leave the table, which can make the dealer feel like he or she is part of the game.

Most dealers work in commercial riverboat or land-based casinos in 11 states: Colorado, Illinois, Indiana, Iowa, Louisiana, Michigan, Mississippi, Missouri, Nevada, New Jersey, and South Dakota. The largest number work in land-based casinos in Nevada, and the second largest number work in similar establishments in New Jersey. Mississippi hires the most dealers on riverboat casinos. In addition, 23 states offer casinos on tribal lands.

Pitfalls

Casino work can be physically demanding, involving long periods of standing, and if you work in a state that allows smoking in the casino you'll be exposed to hazards such as cigarette, cigar, and pipe smoke. Noise from slot machines, gaming tables, and talking workers and patrons may be annoying. Especially at the beginning of your career, you may have to work unpleasant hours, since most casinos are open 24 hours a day, seven days a week, and offer three staggered shifts. Since you must live in the state where you work, you'll be limited in locations, since casinos are only legal in the 11 states listed above.

Perks

The atmosphere in casinos is generally filled with fun and is often considered glamorous. And once your shift is done, that's it—dealers don't have to "take their work home with them" or worry about the job once they're off duty.

Tammy Brathor, blackjack dealer

Dealing blackjack at the MGM Grand in Las Vegas was a good way for Tammy Brathor to earn a living and help support her five boys, aged 7 to 18. Working the graveyard shift (4 a.m. until noon), she juggles motherhood and night school with her five-day-a-week job.

"I love the people I work with," she says. "They're a great group of people. And I meet some interesting people at the hotel, too. Just when you think you've see everything—you haven't!"

Seven years ago, she was working as a pit clerk at the MGM when the company transferred her into the job of dealer, and sent her to school for six weeks to learn blackjack. "I was one of the lucky ones who was already working [at the hotel]," she explains. "Normally, [a dealer] would have to start downtown and work [his or her] way up the strip, to bigger, more popular hotels."

She's been dealing ever since. "A big part of the job is to be personable," she says. "Most of the people are there on vacation, and so you're trying to entertain them. It's important to have a good personality. No one wants to sit in on a game where the dealer is kind of mechanical," she says. "Plus, you get entertained too!"

Initially, all dealers are required to go to school to learn a game. However, once you become a dealer, you can then learn other games just from watching other dealers in-house. "You can observe on your break or after work," she explains. "But my plate is already full!"

There isn't much she doesn't like about her job, except perhaps for the smoky atmosphere. "I'm not a smoker, but I know that inhaling second-hand smoke is part of the job."

If dealing at a Las Vegas casino sounds interesting, Brathor recommends that you'll do well and earn good tips if you can be personable. "I find if you're friendly, most people are personable and friendly back," she says. "There's always one bad apple, but you shouldn't take anything personally. You'll get people who are losing and have consumed alcohol and sometimes they can be a bit verbal. You just ignore it."

Get a Jump on the Job

Get books about different card games and practice dealing. You won't be allowed into a casino until you're at least age 18, but you can read up on the job and practice at home.

CLUB MED HOST

OVERVIEW

If you're the life of the party, the joker with the lampshade on your head, the person always organizing games and activities, you might have what it takes to be a Club Med host (or "G.O."—short for *gentil organisateur* or "friendly host").

Gerard Blitz founded Club Mediterranée as a nonprofit association in 1950, creating a tent village in the Balearic Islands. Seven years later, the first winter village was opened in Leysin, Switzerland. The clubs—popular vacation resorts—have been going strong ever since. They're best known for the "easy living" attitude (you pay up front, and then don't have to shell out money for food, drinks, or activities while you're there).

As a G.O., your job is to make sure Club Med guests have a terrific vacation experience. You'll be welcoming new and returning guests, sharing past experiences, and enjoying all the club's activities right along with the guests. You may gather with guests for a drink or a dance, join them for a gourmet meal at one of the club's restaurants, or perform onstage. As a sort of cross between a host and a companion, the G.O. also may be called upon to provide a variety of other services, including child care, tour guide, front desk, sports, entertainment, and housekeeping.

Job assignments are seasonal, beginning in May for the summer season and November for the winter season; occasionally, jobs may last for less than six months. In general, however, Club Med tries to hire employees for the same village for at least two consecutive seasons.

AT A GLANCE

Salary Range

Former employees report salaries ranging between $400 and $500 a month plus free room and board, free transportation, all the soda you can drink, and free use of the amenities (sailboards, scuba, tennis, snorkeling, and much more).

Education/Experience

There are no set educational requirements, although the ability to speak another language (especially French or Spanish) is a big help. Experience in child care, food service, hospitality, or maintenance is a help.

Personal Attributes

You must be spontaneous and fun loving with a great sense of humor. You need to be flexible, since you won't know where you will be working until you're hired—be it the United States, Mexico, the Caribbean, or the Bahamas. You'll need to be able to function well in a multicultural environment. You must also be willing to participate in club activities and not even mind dressing up in odd costumes. You should enjoy other people and be generous with your time and your friendship.

Requirements

You must be at least 18 with a valid passport; you must also be able to lift at least 30 pounds and be able to relocate for at least six months.

Outlook

Good. These jobs continue to provide vacancies as hosts move from one resort to another, but the club's popularity will ensure there should be plenty of job opportunities through 2012.

If you're interested in exotic locales, Club Med may be for you. There are approximately 120 Club Med villages throughout the world, including villages in Florida and Colorado, Guadeloupe, Bora Bora, Brazil, the Bahamas, the Dominican

Jodie Ortiz, former Club Med host

A Club Med veteran, Jodie Ortiz has been working with the luxury vacation resort for many seasons, working at Turkoise, Turks and Caicos, and Ixtapa, Mexico. Starting out as a boutique salesperson, she moved on to work in a village "circus" program, and then as assistant chief of a village. Currently, Ortiz is a village training coordinator.

Regardless of where you're first hired to work, "you have the chance to learn so many things," Ortiz says. "As a G.O., you have the chance to do all the activities." When Ortiz was first hired right out of university, she worked at a Club Med boutique and then spent some time working at the Club "circus." Some of the Club Med villages offer guests a circus program, with flying trapeze, tightwire, and rope tricks. "In my case I trained for it and actually started to work at the circus. But no matter what you start as, you can always develop an interest in something else. A lot of the G.O.'s do that. Even if you're working in one area, suddenly you get interested in something else."

Ortiz had spent time studying abroad during college, and was interested in other cultures—yet she didn't want to go on her own to live in Mexico. "So I started looking into companies with a little bit of support." She ended up in the boutique in the Sandpiper village in Florida. "When I came straight out of school," she says, "I thought [this job] was a transition, but as it turns out I can't transition away from it!"

As soon as she arrived at Club Med, she felt at home. "It was almost the same setup as a university," she says. "There was something to do during the day, you had a close-knit group of people, young or young-at-heart, you tried a lot of things."

Typically, the Club Med contracts last for six months, and the G.O. will stay in a village for two contracts. However, Ortiz has been at Sandpiper for three and a half years now. Most G.O.s have some kind of skill, she explains. A person working in reception should have had some experience working in reception elsewhere; a G.O. working in child care should have already worked with children or taken a fundamentals course. "Overall," she says, "you have to have skill to be able to speak with people and not be timid. You also learn a lot when you're here, and you get better as you work with it, working with different cultures."

Language courses are very helpful, she adds, because many of the clubs are in foreign countries or attract lots of foreign visitors. Ortiz speaks French, Spanish, and English. "To work in this part of the world, you've got to have English. We're in Florida, and the second language is not primarily Spanish—not all the clientele are Spanish-speaking.

"When you look at a G.O., most of them have some sort of special skills," she says. "Maybe you have a fantastic vocalist or a great dancer. We had a guy on our team who is into Renaissance faires, so we introduced some of that. The broader your interests, the better.

"I thought I would work here a few seasons," she says. "I'm close to 10 years now, and it's become a career. I love it, and I don't have any anticipation of leaving real soon."

Republic, Turks and Caicos, Cancun, and Ixtapa.

Getting the job is the hardest part. You'll have to audition—a four-hour ordeal in which you (and 15 to 25 other candidates) will apply for a variety of positions. During this interview, you'll have to perform a two-minute "audition." You don't need to have a specific talent because what the interviewer wants to see is your personality. You might tell a funny joke or do a card trick. Club Med representatives are always touring new cities looking for exciting talent, and they have local recruiters throughout the country, so you should never be far from a job audition should the fancy strike you.

Pitfalls

It's not all fun and games, of course, especially if you can't deal with ambiguity. You won't know where you're going when you sign up, which is okay if you're adventurous and don't have ties or family. However, other people might prefer a bit more control over their life. You also aren't assured of a job for longer than six months.

Perks

This is a perk-filled job: three meals a day in the restaurants where guests eat plus free soft drinks all day. This means extensive buffet breakfasts and international dishes for lunch and dinner. You'll also be given a room to share (dorm style) and fresh sheets and towels. You'll get medical insurance, and you'll have unlimited use of all amenities on your day off and on your free time. This means you'll get to scuba, snorkel, windsurf, sail, play tennis, lift weights, or just lie around on the beach and get a tan. You also get a 30 percent discount from the Club Med boutique.

Get a Jump on the Job

If you've got talent, work on it, because it may help you land a job during the audition. Read up on Club Med and work on being outgoing and friendly. Try getting some summer jobs as a lifeguard, waitperson, or in any kind of entertainment field.

CONVENTION PLANNER

OVERVIEW

If you've ever attended a large convention (or been in a city when a big convention was in town, with hordes of attendees wearing identical name tags running from one hotel to the next), you'll know that conventions can be a big deal for a company or association. Typically, the convention planner must manage the entire convention with very little support staff, and it's a huge job, involving everything from scheduling enough hotels and renting enough meeting rooms to the nitty-gritty details of making sure each meeting room has the proper foods and beverages and that everyone gets the proper name tag.

Convention planners (also called *meeting planners*) organize conventions, trade shows, reunions, galas, and other kinds of functions for their company or association. A number of people fall into the job because of the experience they gained participating in meetings while holding another job. For example, academics who served on their professional association's meeting planning boards, corporate trainers who had been involved with setting up training sessions, or caterers who routinely served corporate functions—all can move into this profession. They bring their specialized knowledge and education along with their planning experience to the job.

Convention planners work for many different kinds of employers. Corporate planners work for corporations, planning corporate events (usually with the help of many subcontractors). Trade and professional associations hire planners to handle their annual meetings and other functions.

Candy Won, convention planner

When Candy Won started out her career, she had never heard of a convention planner. Instead, she worked in the San Francisco office of a large nonprofit professional association based in Washington, D.C., setting up local arrangements for the association's annual convention. At the time, the association didn't have a full-time planner, but made do with a "local arrangements" committee. But once that San Francisco convention was over, the association—impressed with the job Won did—asked her to move to Washington and take over convention planning full time.

"At that time, they had a consultant," Won says. "I really had no idea that this was an occupation that people were able to do." She's been doing the job ever since—more than 20 years. Today, there are university programs in convention planning, she notes. "But most people in my age group fell into it because of where they worked," she says. "Somebody had to plan a meeting, they became that person, and that's how they got into it." Today it's more of a career track, with courses available and books to read about the profession.

"I like it because it gives you something to aim for, a goal," Won explains. "There's a meeting at the end, and you do see something coming out of your work, rather than just talking about policy." Her association typically requires her to concentrate on planning for their annual convention, although other corporations have a lot more meetings, so their planners are constantly planning one or two meetings a month, small and large.

"The job can get tiring, if you don't want to travel a lot," she says. "A lot of people think it's glamorous, but they're not seeing me crawling around on the floor looking for badge holders. It can be very nitpicky. You've got to get along with people, deal with irate people—it's not a glamorous job."

Because of the size of her association's convention, Won is working on planning meetings through 2013. "Once you settle on a site, [for] seven years from now, contracts have to be dealt with now. But most of the work for a convention is in that particular year, or the year before. Making sure the hotel sets up stuff, and does what they should be doing."

On the other hand, after the meeting is over, Won can sometimes spend an extra few days in a glamorous city, enjoying herself. She enjoys working with a lot of different people every year. "You form friendships, and since there are a limited number of large cities we go to, we'll go back to the same city once in a while."

Hotels and resorts employ planners to handle events booked there; these planners sometimes run events on their own and sometimes work with other planners employed by clients booking the event. Finally, many planners work for independent meeting-planning firms, or destination-management companies.

Regardless of whom they work for, you won't find convention planners sitting behind a desk all day. They visit clients, suppliers, and subcontractors, stay in hotels, and attend functions. They need to be comfortable working in a wide variety of surroundings and with a wide variety of people.

Pitfalls

There can be a fair amount of travel with this job, which may sound glamorous but can become exhausting and tedious. The job also entails enormous stress—typically, you're the one person responsible when the hotel loses the overhead projector and forgets to set up a beverage station at the convention workshop, or if the printer doesn't get the name tags delivered on time.

Perks

Planning conventions can be fun if you truly love juggling lots of responsibilities and travel. You get to visit lots of big cities as part of your job.

Get a Jump on the Job

The more detailed and perfectionist a person you are, the better, so work on your organizational skills while you're still in school. You might consider majoring in hotel management. Consider getting a summer job or internship in a hotel (especially if you can move into convention planning on the hotel side of it). If you know anyone who's attending a convention, see if you can tag along to see what a big convention is all about. This will give you a great idea of the amount of work and number of details there are to be taken care of.

CORPORATE CONCIERGE

OVERVIEW

You're new in a strange city and you need information about the best restaurant within a few blocks of your office. Perhaps you want to impress a client and you need tickets to that impossible-to-get Broadway show. Or maybe you want to hire a limo while you're at work, or you need the name of a great vet to care for your schnauzer and you don't have the time to do it yourself because you're in the middle of closing the biggest deal of your life. It's time to consult your corporate concierge!

Also known as a "lifestyle manager," the corporate concierge exists to arrange special or personal services for clients, manage daily tasks, or simply handle your out-of-control to-do list. Corporate concierges may take messages, arrange for babysitting, make hotel reservations in other cities, give advice about local entertainment or obtain tickets, and monitor requests for housekeeping and maintenance. They may provide information about local and nearby events, sites, historical monuments, and other areas of interest, and recommend great places to eat They may pick up the dry cleaning, relieve the hassle from your personal, business, and domestic life.

Most people think "hotel" when they hear the word *concierge*, but today's corporate concierges are professional lifestyle managers who provide time-saving services for busy individuals and businesses worldwide. A corporate concierge is sort of like your very own affordable personal assistant to help manage your life so that you can get more done each day. Services might in-

clude personal shopping, fetching your dry cleaned clothes, or booking your holidays. Your personal assistant takes care all those things that you'd rather not do—or don't have time to do. Typically, a corporate concierge working for a company would receive a nominal fee from the company based on number of employees; after that, there's an hourly fee payable either by the employee (for each task requested) or by the company.

Pitfalls

Sometimes clients can be difficult, needy, and grumpy. The concierge typically stands

---

AT A GLANCE

Salary Range

$12 to $15+ per hour (more for large corporate clients), plus tips and incentives such as commissions. Tips can be substantial and make up a good part of your income.

Education/Experience

Customer service background is helpful; business experience is also helpful.

Personal Attributes

You should be friendly and knowledgeable of the city and its venues. You should also be professional, detail-oriented, a team player, able to work well under pressure and in a fast-paced environment.

Requirements

Good written and oral communication skills; attention to detail; excellent telephone etiquette; computer literate. Knowledge of several languages is helpful in large, big-city hotels.

Outlook

Growing. While traditional concierge jobs are often available in large cities across the country, more and more opportunities are becoming available for corporate concierges in many more cities.

Sara-Ann Kasner, corporate concierge

When Sara-Ann Kasner started out, she was aiming for a career as an office manager, but life has a funny way of taking turns. About 14 years ago she traded in her real estate job for a stint as a concierge, and she's never looked back.

Today, Kasner is the director of the Just for You Concierge Services, a division of the Zeller Realty Group. As a corporate concierge, she offers services to a tenant base of about 10,000 office workers throughout the Twin Cities area and Chicago. Kasner is also the founder of the National Concierge Association.

"I've been a concierge in a corporate office setting for about 14 years," she says. "I've been quite successful as a concierge in the Twin Cities of Minneapolis and St. Paul and have been upwardly mobile in my profession since I started."

Kasner attended the University of Minnesota business school, and studied broadcast journalism. She's worked at everything from newscaster at a small market radio station in northern Minnesota to selling real estate and managing a real estate office in the metropolitan Minneapolis area. "Feeling a little burned out in real estate, I answered an ad for a 'corporate concierge' in an office tower in Minneapolis," she says. "To my surprise, they offered me a position in which I was to create a concierge service for the property management firm that managed that building. In every way I felt it was entrepreneurial, and an opportunity to create a worthwhile service for busy office workers."

As a corporate concierge, her services range from obtaining tickets to the theater, to snagging restaurant reservations, managing floral deliveries, helping out with weekend plans, client entertainment, tenant appreciation events, personal event planning, and some light errand services.

In 1993, Kasner joined a local group called the Twin Cities Concierge Association. "I set out to enhance and increase my networking opportunities by convincing others to join our group, and I petitioned the group to permit a variety of venues to also join—not just concierges." She discovered there were a variety of concierge services sprouting up in the Twin Cities and every facet of the hospitality industry, and all of them wanted to network. "Networking is the key to our success since I, as a concierge professional, am too busy servicing my clients to be everywhere all of the time and keep up with the trends in the industry. It became clear to me that I needed a team of experts in my hip pocket to maintain my success." As a result, she came up with the organizational concept of networking across the nation.

In 1997, she invited a group of concierges from across the country to join her for a brainstorming weekend in Minneapolis, which turned into the National Concierge Association (NCA). Today the group has more than 600 members worldwide, with local chapters throughout the United States, Canada, and Japan. "The result is that no matter what request is posed by my clients, I can accomplish miracles based on my contacts everywhere." She's been able to produce a bottle of wine delivered within minutes of the request in downtown San Diego, hard-to-come-by tickets to a museum in Holland, a last-minute car rental in London. She even managed to track down a request for a rare book.

"What I love best about my job is the variety," she says. "No two days are ever the same and I never know what is going to be requested of me each day. I now have staff to support my services and we are all extremely busy."

and must be on his or her feet for long hours at a time. Most concierges work from 7 a.m. to 3 p.m. or from 3 p.m. to 11 p.m., and weekend work is almost a given.

Perks

The tips can be great; many times a guest, group, or family will give the concierge something in exchange for good information and service. If you love people, enjoy tracking down information, and have lots of connections in your city, this can be a great job. You may interact with individuals from all over the world.

Get a Jump on the Job

Study hard in school and try to learn at least one other language, since speaking several languages can be a real boon to a corporate concierge. Think about studying hotel management in college; at the very least, try to get a summer job as a bellhop or in the hotel business, or with a real estate management company.

CRUISE SHIP ACTIVITY DIRECTOR

OVERVIEW

If you've ever spent a rainy Sunday immersed in old *Love Boat* reruns, you'll know all about the job of a cruise ship activity director (or *cruise ship director*). It looks like a fun job making sure everyone else on board is having a good time, and it can be enjoyable—but there's also plenty of hard work involved. Most large ships are sort of like floating five-star hotels with lavish meals, terrific entertainment, and all kinds of sports, fitness, and spa activities. Basically, as a cruise director, you'll be responsible for all of the onboard entertainment and making sure all the guests are having a good time.

There's no standard type of cruise director however, because every cruise line is a little bit different and expects different things of its activities directors. This being the case, the best way for you to learn the job is to get hired on a cruise as an assistant cruise director or staff member and watch what the cruise director does.

No matter what other duties the director might have, most cruises expect the cruise director to help entertain the guests and usually to perform a few times per voyage. Cruise directors were once the primary entertainer on board a cruise, but today they have more administrative responsibilities and fewer performing responsibilities. They supervise the cruise staff activities department. They also chat up the guests during cocktail parties, organize impromptu shuffleboard games, and call out bingo numbers on the Lido deck. On many cruise lines, you'll also find the cruise director herding guests together for different tours, sometimes leading tours, and also acting in a public relations capacity from time to time.

In this job, longevity counts; cruise ships reward employees who have the skills needed to work with passengers (who can sometimes be demanding or difficult) by hiring from within the current list of outstanding crew members.

When your contract begins, you'll usually be expected to pony up the money to get to the ship—but often, you'll receive an airline ticket back home at the end of your contract if you've fulfilled your end of the bargain. If the cruise line liked your work, you'll usually be offered another contract (plus plane ticket) back to the ship after being at home for six to eight weeks. However, if you quit or get fired before the contract is up, you'll have to pay your own way back home.

Pitfalls

Accommodations are sometimes cramped, especially on smaller vessels, and you may be sharing your cabin with little or no privacy. If you decide that you just can't stand shipboard life another minute and you break your contract, you'll have to pay for all costs to get yourself home.

If long-range planning is your bane, you won't do well on a cruise line, because most companies require a four- to six-month commitment. Although some cruise lines will let you take vacation during this period, others won't. If you sign on and you don't like the ship—you're stuck. Workdays are long—often 12 to 14 hours, and you'll usually find yourself working for many weeks in a row with no time off. Personal space is also an issue; most workers share very small, windowless cabins. Even on a large luxury ship,

your world will start to shrink after spending weeks on board with no time off and no energy left to enjoy time off even if you do get it. Typically people work for four to six weeks in a row before getting two weeks off.

And while you'll get free room and board and medical coverage while working on the ship, you'll lose all these benefits as soon as you have time off. Although it may sound great to work without having to pay your rent, the gas bill, and the garbage pickup fee while on board, most people still need to keep some sort of home on shore. This means you're still stuck with those bills for your home base, and the relatively low salaries don't stretch that far.

Perks

If you've got a yen to travel, then cruising could be the best job for you, since as a cruise director you can sail all over the world while also getting free room and board. As a cruise employee, you'll get to visit all kinds of fascinating places, and your contract should allow you a certain amount of time off the ship (it's a negotiable item). Most cruise lines allow their crew members to prowl around the ports until an hour or two before departure, unless they've pulled on-ship duty. Another benefit: your bank account. Since there's nowhere much to go most of the time, you'll be able to save most of the money you earn—your room and board is covered, after all. Some cruise ships even give you a bar allowance. On your days off, you're allowed to hang around by the pool, catch some rays, or relax in the spa. Some ships provide in-room crew TVs, special crew lounges and recreation areas, not to mention your own Internet connections and computer lounges. Also,

John Heald, cruise ship activity director

John Heald considers himself very lucky to have snagged a job on a cruise ship with the Carnival Cruise Line. "I had started in the beverage department and eventually became a social host," he explains. "This is a position responsible for hosting many of the activities on board, including deck games, bingo, quizzes, and many other shipboard events." Eventually, Heald worked his way up to become a cruise director. "When I first started, I was responsible for 25 staff," he says, "but as the ships have grown in size, so have the cruise director's responsibilities. I'm now responsible for a staff of 70 staff dancers, performers, musicians, and other staff members. I was very lucky to find something I enjoy so much!"

He's been at sea with Carnival as a cruise director since 1991. "I've worked on most of Carnival Cruise Lines' ships and have been responsible for seven new ship launches, including my current posting on the Carnival *Liberty*.

"The best part of my job is the reward of making people laugh and knowing that their valuable vacation time has been enhanced by the activity and entertainment program you've given them," Heald says. "When a guest returns to a ship and says: 'We have come back just to see you'—that's worth a million dollars. The cruise director is the one person who can affect the guest's vacation more than anyone."

But working on board ship as activity director isn't always easy. Although getting paid for endless travel may sound exciting and romantic at first, as you get older the gloss begins to wear. Cruise directors with families find it difficult to be away from home for the extended periods necessary for a cruise. "My least favorite part of the job is being away from my family," Heald agrees. "Anyone who travels away to work will say the same. It is the hardest part of working on the ocean." Other cruise directors also note that when the ship is in port and the weather doesn't cooperate, if you're a guest you can just go back to bed and take a nap. The activity director is suddenly faced with a ship full of cranky passengers to entertain. This is when the team must pull together to make the day happen with a whole new program of events and activities.

Although working aboard a floating pleasure palace may seem ideal to most people, it's still a job with its own limitations and frustrations. It takes a special kind of person to handle living over the shop. You must like people, and because you work with your colleagues 24-7 and you're in front of the public for up to 18 hours a day, you can't fake it.

Although most cruise lines do not require any specific background or education, Heald recommends that you love all things entertainment if you want to be a cruise director. "You have to love being the center of attention and have the ability to realize you can never have a bad day at work! Once you walk out of your cabin door, you have to portray the 'fun' that the cruise line advertised which got the passengers to book the cruise in the first place. It is a totally unique job and can be the most rewarding job in the world. I wouldn't have missed the journey for anything."

if you're one of those people who like to work hard for a certain period and then have long stretches off between work periods to follow your own interests, this job might be ideal.

Get a Jump on the Job

Since many cruise director jobs require some kind of entertainment background, you might think about getting some experience or training in singing, acting, or dancing. Read everything you can about cruising, and see if you can take a short cruise to see what life at sea is all about.

Although there are lots of Web sites and books that say they'll help you get a cruise job, the best way to look for a cruise director job is by visiting the official cruise line Web sites. You can read all about available jobs, qualifications, and how to apply. Avoid a fee-based cruise placement agency—legitimate placement agencies almost never charge money for their services.

GOLF COURSE SUPERINTENDENT

OVERVIEW

Golf course superintendents are like baseball umpires; if nobody notices them, they're probably doing a great job. The course must be in such good shape that even golfers shooting 90 can find nobody to blame for their poor scores but themselves. But if golfers start gossiping about their superintendent, it usually means the grass is diseased or has too many bare spots. If there's a tournament going on, players may complain that the greens are too fast or the pin placements, or location of the holes, are too difficult. Superintendents try their best to avoid complaints. They are notorious for being conscientious, introverted, and taking the condition of their courses personally. Look around at your neighbors who are the fussiest about their lawns—then multiply their dedication by 10 and you have a golf course superintendent.

Most superintendents get to work by 6 a.m. to organize their staff and prepare the course. Depending upon a facility's size, there may be just a few assistants, or a staff of 50.

The superintendent makes sure that the grass is cut to the desired length, that the bunkers are raked and the holes and tee markers are regularly moved so one spot doesn't get worn out. The superintendent makes sure there's always enough water on the grass. Although the course usually gets watered every evening, strong winds during the night may leave the course so dry in the morning that even more water is needed. And this is just the routine maintenance! Superintendents spend endless hours checking their courses for grass diseases or pests and other problems that can get quickly out of hand. Many superintendents have college degrees in turf grass management or agronomy. More than 100 colleges and universities offer two- or four-year programs in one of these fields. Many other superintendents have majored in business because they're expected to help their course or club keep down expenses. Superintendents help save money by taking care of projects that otherwise would have to be done by outside contractors.

Pat Finlen, golf course superintendent

Pat Finlen is such a stickler for detail that he puts his entire staff at Olympic Club in San Francisco through an early-morning stretching routine. Finlen, at his daily 5:30 a.m. staff meeting, hands out assignments, makes announcements, and warms up some 50 employees with basic exercises. "Otherwise, most people roll right out of bed into physical activity," he says. "Some of these guys will be on a mower for eight hours."

His attention to detail helps explain why Finlen was hired to oversee one of the nation's most famous golf clubs, which includes two 18-hole and a nine-hole course. His work at the Bayonet and Black Horse Course on the Monterey Peninsula south of San Francisco led to his hiring at Olympic Club. "To get a better job, you've got to have good playing conditions," he says. "That's what everybody sees." At a club, members are always bringing guests, Finlen explains, and a member might tell the guest your name. "That's what gets you noticed," he says. "Then you sell yourself on business skills, financial skills, and communication skills. And that's where a lot of superintendents lose their jobs—not because of turf issues, but because of other problems. They can grow the greatest grass, but if they can't communicate, a little problem becomes a bigger one."

Finlen understands that his club members don't want to be the last ones to know about a problem on the course. If they notice an obvious difficulty, he wants them to know he's dealing with it. "You have to have good communication with your membership," Finlen says. "If members go out and play golf and see a bad area and they don't have a response in 24 hours, they'll wonder what's going on. Every week, I send out an e-mail to every committee member and let them know what we're doing on the golf course and I'll probably get seven or eight replies. A lot of times, they just want to know what's going on and they just want to be heard."

Because golf superintendents put their hearts and souls into their jobs, they take criticism of their courses quite personally. Most are their own toughest critics. "I remember having some greens that

---

Plumbing, electrical, or minor construction work, for instance, usually is done by a superintendent and his crew. When a contractor is needed for bigger jobs, such as rebuilding a bunker or draining a lake, the superintendent supervises the work.

Whether superintendents work for a municipal course or exclusive club, they're wise to keep their bosses and golfers informed about problems or projects on the course. As superintendents get around their courses, they'll find that golfers aren't shy about remarking whether they consider playing conditions to be excellent or shabby. Yet, a superintendent usually remains anonymous outside the course, unless it's

host to an big tournament. Then, the superintendent may find that players, fans, and the media become intensely interested in his work. Superintendents actually have turned into celebrities at high-profile tournaments such as the U.S. Open. The U.S. Golf Association, which runs the Open, is famous for preparing extremely difficult courses, highlighted by narrow fairways, deep rough, very fast greens, and difficult pin placements. Players complain that U.S. Open courses actually are unfair, so at a U.S. Open, the course sometimes gets as much attention as the players. That's when superintendents find themselves besieged by reporters. Once the U.S. Open, or another did not do well during the summer," Finlen says. "They had a disease and I was treating it, but I was sick to my stomach for six weeks. You take it so personally because that is you out on the golf course. When you drive around and see golfers, there's nothing better than seeing smiles on their faces and hear them saying that the course has never been better. Conversely, nothing's worse than driving around and knowing, even though it wasn't your fault, that conditions aren't what they should be."

Finlen broke into the golf business at a pro shop in Lake Quivira, Kansas. He then took a maintenance job there on weekends and, after earning a business degree, tried to apply what he'd learned about grass to the landscaping business. But when that didn't work out, he went back to golf.

He regularly attends seminars on turf management given by the Golf Course Superintendents Association of America. He also could have used a few seminars from Bob Vila, because he's had to become something of a handyman, too. "This job has become more business-oriented than it ever was," Finlen says. "Once, the superintendent just wanted to grow grass, get his budget, and be left alone. Now we're the go-to guys to get something done. If revenues are down, superintendents have to be very creative solving problems and making repairs rather than just saying, 'We'll go hire a contractor.' "

Finlen received one of his biggest challenges when the Olympic Club was awarded the 2012 U.S. Open. For an open, however, preparing the course is just one part of a superintendent's job. There must be accommodations for parking lots, dozens of corporate tents and facilities for volunteers, media, security, and emergency personnel. Once the tournament is over, the cleanup job is immense. Finlen doesn't seem daunted by all the potential headaches.

"The U.S. Open is like the Super Bowl of your career," he says. "All the other stuff is just part of the territory."

big tournament, is over, the superintendent can go back to being anonymous. And that's just the way most superintendents like it.

Pitfalls

Twelve-hour days are routine, and you're always at the mercy of Mother Nature. Too much heat and humidity can make your greens as hard as rock. The condition of your course is constantly scrutinized and sometimes criticized, so your work is constantly being assessed.

Perks

As a superintendent, you're working outdoors most of the time and spending your time around a sport you probably love. You can make an excellent income and enjoy a very long career.

Get a Jump on the Job

You can start playing golf as early as you get the urge. As you're going around a course, take a good look at how it is maintained. While you're still in high school, you might be able to get a golf course job, mowing grass or performing other maintenance. If you have a lawn, get involved in growing grass and learn about blends of grass, growing conditions, weeds, pests, and turf diseases.

HUMAN CANNONBALL

OVERVIEW

Have you ever thought you'd like to become an astronaut but you don't really want to leave planet Earth? You could always become a human cannonball, the ultimate circus daredevil. When you get shot out of a cannon, you'll feel the kind of g-force that astronauts experience when they accelerate or decelerate quickly. As a human cannonball, you'll experience seven times the ordinary pull of gravity. In fact, it's so rough that some performers take space training to learn to withstand the forces.

But getting shot out of the cannon is only the *start* of the act. Once you pop out, you're propelled up to 65 miles an hour in half a second, flying 40 feet high and more than 120 feet before you land on an airbag. Unlike an astronaut, however, you may have to do this 10 times a week.

This act is so mind-boggling that many believe there's trickery involved. Peggy Williams, education outreach manager for the Ringling Bros. and Barnum & Bailey Circus, was once offered money to let a bystander get shot out of a cannon—but this definitely isn't something for amateurs. A first-timer would be lucky to survive with a few broken bones. Even the professionals aren't always that lucky.

When you put your life into the hands of a machine, you don't want to leave anything to chance. A top-notch human cannonball will hire an engineer to design a cannon, then build it himself in a machine shop. A performer will regularly test the cannon's safety and accuracy by shooting

AT A GLANCE

Salary Range

Trade secret! Human cannonballs guard their trade secrets as closely as do magicians. They don't want to reveal their salaries because that might encourage new competition.

Education/Experience

A circus school can introduce you to the basics of being a human cannonball. Many cannonballs started in flying trapeze or other aerial acts.

Personal Attributes

You'll need extreme dedication because the top human cannonballs spend a great deal of time practicing and maintaining their cannons. You'll need to be fearless and able to perform despite injuries, bumps, and bruises.

Requirements

You'll need acrobatic skills and must be in terrific shape. Excess weight will make it harder for you to fly through the air. You'll also need to have your own cannon.

Outlook

There usually are fewer than a dozen human cannonballs in the nation, so these jobs are scarce. And when jobs come open, there are performers lining up for them. Nothing is easy about becoming a cannonball and that includes finding a job.

out a dummy. Once you've tested the cannon a few times and practiced your act, it's show time.

The cannon's barrel is big enough for you to stand almost erect, since you're tilted to a 45-degree angle. Then your assistant fires the cannon and you'll explode into the air and fly like Superman, with your arms out to the side. Unlike Superman, however, you won't land on your feet. You'll flip in the air and hit the airbag while flat on your back. If everything goes

Brian and Tina Miser, human cannonballs

Even after a decade as a human cannonball, Brian Miser still feels tense every time the five-second countdown begins. "It's always very stressful mentally," he says. "You start to slide down the cannon and you get inside and all you see is the ceiling of the arena, and it looks like you're going to hit it. Your heart starts thumping and you get to one, and it's pounding harder. They say, 'Fire!' and the next thing you know, you're flying out."

This act seems so implausible that Miser is often asked if there's a trick. Some ask if he has a twin who somehow winds up in the airbag while he stays in the cannon. But in fact, Miser doesn't have a twin—although he does have a wife, Tina, who gets shot out of a cannon with him for Ringling Bros. and Barnum & Bailey Circus. They were the first duo to try this act in more than 30 years, and the first to line up behind one another instead of side by side. "She flies a little bit shorter than I do and I fly over the top of her," Miser explained. "If the timing's off between the releases, there's a chance I'm going to hit her because she's going to be right in my path. There's about a three-tenths of second difference."

They also perform high falls, diving from 45 feet into an airbag. "I've done most of the circus thrill acts," Brian says. "I always liked the challenge and danger—facing up to the fear."

As much as he enjoys the challenge, he was reluctant to let Tina join the cannonball act. She was pregnant and had been injured in her previous cannon shot. "She broke her collarbone, landing in the airbag," Miser recalls. "She didn't have a good flight." Frightened after her accident, it was some time before she wanted to get back into the cannon and rejoin the act.

Tina had been operating Brian's cannon since 1999. Both grew up in Peru, Indiana, and learned circus skills as part of a youth circus program. Each summer, about 1,000 adult volunteers and young performers between ages 8 and 21 put on a well-known circus in Peru. (The town once served as winter headquarters for several circus troupes.)

Brian was a circus star in Peru and after graduating from high school he performed at Circus World and for Ringling Bros. He then went out on his own and formed the Flying Eagles, who performed internationally. Tina had also set her sights on the flying trapeze once she graduated from high school a few years after Brian. But her parents insisted she attend college, and she graduated from Ball State University. She also served in the Air Force Reserves before she returned to Peru in 1999 and became a circus volunteer. At the time, Brian was home recovering from an injury, working on a new act, and also helping out with the circus. He'd been a trapeze artist for 14 years, but wanted a new challenge and taught himself to be a human cannonball. With an engineer's help, he even taught himself how to build a cannon. He asked Tina to join him on the road and operate his cannon.

"You don't get that offer many days," she says. Brian proposed marriage while they were flying a powered parachute over a house they were building in Peru. "I had the ring tied to my belt loop so I wouldn't drop it," he says.

Early in their marriage, Brian developed an act, Bailey's Comet, which became part of the Ringling Bros. grand finale. He lit himself on fire before Tina fired him across the arena floor. "I was the first and only one to do that—the only one stupid enough to do that," he says. "I landed and stood and burned for 15 to 20 seconds and they would extinguish me." During that tour, the Misers had a daughter, Skyler—a Norse name that means projectile.

"She loves the circus," Brian says. "If she wants to be a cannonball, I'll teach her. She'll learn to count from five to one backwards before she learns to count forward."

right, you'll accept wild applause and look ahead to the next show. If anything goes wrong, you might be on your way to the hospital.

Human cannonballs have been a small and select group since William Hunt, a Canadian high-wire performer known as "The Great Farini," first patented a device for launching "human projectiles" in 1871. The device wasn't actually a cannon and used rubber springs, which propelled a young man, "Lulu," 40 feet into the air in 1873. George Loyal, of the Yankee Robinson Circus, was the first person ever fired out of a cannon in 1875. The act's popularity faded in the 1890s, but was revived in the 1920s when Europeans built a better cannon. Ildebrando Zacchini, patriarch of a family circus act, built a cannon powered by compressed air that made a loud and smoky explosion. Circus owner John Ringling brought the Zacchinis to the United States in 1929, and sons Mario and Emanuel invented a double cannon that fired two people in rapid succession. Emanuel Zacchini once flew 175 feet, a world record until David Smith, Sr. flew 180 feet, four inches at Manville, New Jersey, in 1995. He broke his own record in 1998 by flying 185 feet, 10 inches.

Pitfalls

This is not a career for the faint of heart. You can get seriously injured being shot out of a cannon. You'll also have to deal with a grueling schedule—as many as 10 shows a week for most of the year. You're constantly on the move and seldom get home.

Perks

Cannonballs enjoy the challenge and independent lifestyle of their unique job. They can make an excellent living and enjoy the satisfaction of being among a small group of people in the entire world able to perform their feat.

Get a Jump on the Job

You might try gymnastics to learn how to fly through the air. Serious students usually attend circus school or become human cannonballs after performing other high-risk acts, such as the flying trapeze.

ICE RINK MANAGER

OVERVIEW

Do you love executing a perfect triple toe loop? Do you get a thrill from smacking a puck past an aggressive goalie? Do you just love the frosty atmosphere of an ice rink? If this strikes your fancy, managing an ice rink might be the right job for you. Keep in mind, however, that you won't be able to kick back and wait for customers to flood into your rink—you've got to get out there and hustle up business. Expenses are very high and profits can be low, so the more you can do to boost your bottom line, the better. Peak business is limited mostly to evenings and weekends.

A rink manager must be creative in selling as many hours of ice for as many activities as possible. A team or club can rent an hour of ice for about $250 in the Midwest, but that same ice might cost at least twice as much on the east coast. Youngsters are a rink's best customers, so most managers will develop ice hockey and figure skating organizations while offering recreational skating, too. A popular youth hockey organization might have 500 or more players. A rink may also have a spot for indoor or outdoor roller hockey. Some rinks pack in recreational skaters during holiday seasons, using popular music and special lighting to attract teenagers. Rinks can also appeal to older customers by organizing adult hockey leagues or sponsoring broom hockey games between local organizations. Most rinks also have rooms that can be rented for birthday parties, business meetings, or other events.

AT A GLANCE

Salary Range
$35,000 to $120,000

Education/Experience
You should have a college degree or have taken some college courses, preferably in business. Many rink managers have run a small business or a youth sports organization.

Personal Attributes
You should have a passion for ice sports, and you must enjoy people so you can make everybody at your rink feel welcome. You must also interact well with youngsters, because they're your best customers.

Requirements
You should be familiar with hockey, figure skating, and other ice sports, which will boost your credibility and help you understand your customers' needs.

Outlook
Jobs are most plentiful in traditional winter sports areas, but successful rinks have also sprouted up in such Sunbelt states as California, Florida, and Arizona. Rinks are often not highly profitable, however, and their numbers aren't expected to increase significantly over the next several years.

If a rink has more than one sheet of ice, it can generate additional business, but it will also have higher expenses. Ice time is expensive because a rink's utility bills and repairs are expensive. This is why managing a rink is such a challenge. An ice rink may seem pretty simple when you think of a pond freezing over during winter. But indoor rinks require cooling, maintenance, and equipment. The electric, gas, and water bills are huge. A Zamboni (the vehicle used to resurface

Dave Groulx, ice rink manager

Canadian Dave Groulx graduated from Cornell University and spent nine years as an engineer for John Deere—but ice hockey was in his heart, and his mind was never far from the sport. Eventually, Groulx gave in to the pull of the ice, and he took a job as rink manager first in West Palm Beach, Florida, and then in Shawnee, Kansas.

A native of Welland, Ontario, he played hockey at Cornell and had a few professional tryouts, and while working for John Deere, Groulx coached junior hockey teams in Ontario, just across the border from Buffalo, New York. Junior hockey teams are made up of former high school players who hope to earn college scholarships or get noticed by professional teams.

Groulx also started a sporting goods store and bought a slow-pitch softball complex. In 1992 he bought the Lakeland Ice Warriors, a minor league team in the Sunshine Hockey League. Groulx served as the team's owner, general manager, coach, and marketing director. He also formed a youth hockey organization, which he hoped would grow with the pro team's popularity. Instead, the youth organization was more successful than the pro team. Groulx still keeps a framed photo of the Ice Warriors in his office at Ice Sports in Shawnee, Kansas. That photo and a dozen jerseys were the only returns on his investment, before he sold the team after three seasons. "The hockey business is very difficult," Groulx says. "There are more sad stories than success stories in the hockey world."

Nevertheless, Groulx wasn't daunted by one sad story. He took over a rink in West Palm Beach, Florida, overseeing a busy operation that included 52 youth and adult hockey teams. Then, in 2002, he was hired by a Canadian company to become manager and minority owner of the Ice Sports rink in Shawnee. That rink had failed under two previous owners and was competing against three other rinks in a tight market. Groulx promoted youth hockey at Ice Sports by merging his association with another in the area. When the owner expressed interest in selling the rink, Groulx recruited new ownership and kept Ice Sports on its feet. He achieved that through his love of hockey, a knack for developing business and personal relationships, and a lot of hard work.

"You need a passion to do this," Groulx says. "It's a minimum 70-hour-a-week job and you'd better like working weekends. Anybody who thinks this is a nine-to-five job better look elsewhere."

Groulx performs three or four jobs rolled into one. "My alarm doesn't have to go off in the morning," he says. "I look forward to getting up every day. I don't know how many people can say that. Every day's different because I wear most of the hats around here." He oversees sales and staffing at the pro shop and snack bar, and he keeps an eye on maintenance and stays alert for unpleasant surprises.

Groulx puts his personal stamp on the rink by knowing most customers on a first-name basis. "You need to make people feel welcome," he says. "You need to make them feel like someone when they walk in. You have to be like McDonald's—the kids have to be dragging their parents into the rink." Rink managers also should be visible, friendly, and respected. "If you're a hockey guy," he says, "you should've played the game so you're able to tell the tall tales."

the ice) is expensive to buy and repair. Then there are the locker rooms, which often need to be painted, repaired, or expanded. Nearly any rink repair costs at least $1,000. Bringing in enough business to cover these expenses isn't easy.

If you're managing a large, successful rink, you'll be able to hire a full staff, including an operations manager to supervise maintenance and new projects, a sales manager to book the ice, a hockey director, a figure skating director, a pro shop manager, a concessions manager, and a supervisor for each work shift. Few ice rink managers have the luxury of a complete staff, however, and they usually perform several jobs themselves. This requires a lot of time and know-how, which is why a rink manager probably should have a college degree and a good head for business.

A manager can count on keeping a rink busy during the fall and winter, the prime seasons for winter sports. But the bills don't stop coming in the spring and summer, which is why a manager must find ways to keep a rink busy all year. Most rinks offer a heavy schedule of ice hockey during the spring and summer—leagues, tournaments, clinics, and drop-in sessions.

To publicize all these activities, managers often maintain a Web site and send out flyers or brochures to keep interest in the rink high. If a hockey league or figure skating club that uses the rink is run by an independent organization, the rink manager works with coaches, parents, board members and players to make sure everybody involved is having a good time.

Pitfalls

Rink managers work long hours and are busiest during evenings and weekends. Rinks are often unprofitable, and a manager may feel under pressure to please the owner. Repairs, maintenance, and security present constant headaches.

Perks

Most rink managers love what they're doing. They enjoy being around ice sports and the people who coach and participate in them. They also enjoy the variety of challenges and responsibilities.

Get a Jump on the Job

If you participate in hockey, figure skating, or another ice sport, you'll probably have a good idea what facilities and services a rink should provide. You can get a part-time or summer job working behind the snack bar or helping to keep the rink clean, which can help you get a bird's eye view of the job.

IMAGE CONSULTANT

OVERVIEW

The unfortunate job seeker who pairs a woolen sweater with a shapeless suit and uses the wrong fork during a luncheon interview is in desperate need of help—from an image consultant.

An image consultant is a specialist who can help you shop for a new work wardrobe, suggest ways to improve your habitual slouch, or jazz up your drooping hairstyle. Since the popularity of TV makeover shows like *Extreme Makeover*, the image consultant career is becoming better known every day. Today, there are about 1,000 of these consultants in the United States. About three-quarters of their clients are looking for advice to boost their careers.

The typical image consultant specializes in visual appearance and verbal and nonverbal communication. An image consultant counsels individual and corporate clients on appearance, behavior, and communication skills through individual consultations, coaching, presentations, seminars, and workshops.

An image consultant could help a mid-level account executive who feels stuck in her career, assisting her with buying some new clothes in brand-new shades and styles. A typical consultant might charge $500 for three sessions, in addition to between $500 and $1,000 for a one-day shopping trip, may make suggestions about hairstyles and eyeglass frames, and can evaluate the overall impression a client makes by studying verbal and physical communication styles.

Image consultants may refer clients to cosmetic dentists, vocal coaches, or plastic surgeons, while others focus mostly on clothes. Some corporate-image consultants hone in on business-related issues, such as

Ginger Burr, image consultant

Ginger Burr was busy working as a word processor at the Massachusetts Institute of Technology when she realized that she didn't want to spend her work life in a virtual cubicle. "I was thinking, 'This is not what I want to do with my life,'" she recalls. "I knew I wanted to own my own business, and I knew I preferred working with women." A former modeling school student, she'd always enjoyed fashion and makeup.

But this was 20 years ago, when no one really had ever heard of an "image consultant." Then came the day she attended a seminar on color and makeup and style. "I ate it up," she recalls. "I knew I had the interest, but I didn't really know what image consulting was. Back then, there wasn't even an association for image consultants."

She went home and started right away, working on style and colors with her friends. "I practiced on them," she says. Starting out part time, her business steadily grew through word of mouth and she was able to start cutting her hours at MIT as her business prospered.

In 1987, Burr launched her company, Total Image Consultants, with the belief that a dynamic personal and professional image could be created without having to give up your own personal style or comfort. She's built her career as an expert personal image consultant and makeup artist, and a leader in the field of fashion and style.

Burr offers private consultations and makeovers for men, women, teenagers, brides-to-be, and transgender clients. She also directs corporate seminars and community education programs for some of Boston's most prestigious organizations including investment companies, law firms, and Harvard Law School.

She's the past president of the New England Chapter of the Association of Image Consultants International (AICI) and has served on the AICI's International Board as the vice president of member communications, and she's the author of *Fashion Secrets Mother Never Taught You.*

Today, the path to being an image consultant is a little simpler: You can go to college and major in image consulting. For example, the Fashion Institute of Technology in New York City offers a four-year degree in this field. It's important to get training and to be aware of the fact that image consulting is a very broad profession. "There are a lot of different things that fall under its umbrella, so it's important to find out what parts you like," Burr says. "Most image consultants have their own businesses, so you'll need to be persistent and learn about business in general. If you don't learn about business and just go with what you think is fun, you won't make it."

There are the occasional rough spots when business slows down, but it always picks up again, she says. "Some times of the year are busier than others. And of course, there isn't a steady paycheck, but I've kind of gotten used to that.

"I made a lot of mistakes when I started out," Burr says. For one thing, she ran an expensive print ad in *Boston Magazine* that cost a lot of money but didn't bring in that much business. Instead, what worked for her was to offer free makeovers at her hair stylist's salon. "That got me in front of a number of people," she says. "Back then, I didn't know about networking." Since then, she's joined women's networking associations and learned how to network and introduce her business to other people.

"I like the variety," she says. "I do so many things in my business and everything is different. I love seeing the transformation in women, how much easier I can make their life, building self-esteem. I also love working for myself, and I love fashion and makeup and all that goes along with it."

visual and verbal communication during presentations.

Consultants generally help clients modernize their wardrobe, keeping only stylish clothes that fit well and complement their coloring. Consultants also offer a variety of other services to clients including ballroom dancing, makeup, personal shopping, etiquette, speech and diction, and corporate seminars.

Pitfalls

It can be stressful to have to maintain a positive, upbeat image with difficult clients. You may need to work very long or unpredictable hours.

Perks

If you love clothes, have lots of style, and truly enjoy other people, you can have a ball with this highly paid profession. And the better you do, the more referrals you'll have—so the sky's the limit.

Get a Jump on the Job

Learn as much as you can about personal style, clothing, and hair. See if you can get an internship or summer job at a department store or boutique, working with a clothing buyer or a store's "personal shopper."

LIMOUSINE DRIVER

OVERVIEW

Booked on an early-morning flight but don't have time to park your car at the long-distance parking lot? You need a limousine. Want to impress your prom date? You and your friends might chip in to hire a limo. Or maybe you're nominated for an Oscar and you want to arrive at the Academy Awards show in style—so you hire a limousine.

Cabs and car services may provide fine transportation, but if you want to get someplace in style, a limousine is the only answer. Limousine companies may be owned by one person, a family, or a large company with from one to a fleet of vehicles. When you think of a limousine service, you usually think of a stretch limo with a wet bar, TV set, DVD system, and tinted glass. But limousine services also offer town cars, vans, SUVs, and buses—and each and every one needs a trained driver.

To be hired as a limousine driver, you typically need to be at least 25 years old with a stable background and good driving record. If you've had more than a few traffic violations or accidents, you don't belong in this business. If you don't enjoy dealing with the public, you don't belong in this business, either. Most limousine companies, in fact, consider it easier to teach a new driver how to operate the extra-long car than it is to teach how to give excellent service. For instance, a limousine

AT A GLANCE

Salary Range
$35,000 to $80,000

Education/Experience
You'll need the reading skills of any licensed driver. Experience as a professional driver is a plus, though many companies require training for all new drivers, even those who've worked as drivers elsewhere.

Personal Attributes
You should be service-minded, because pleasing the customer is the key to success in this business. You must also be reliable and stable; a driver who behaves irresponsibly or shows up late won't last long.

Requirements
Many companies will want you to be at least 25 years old, because by that age, drivers are usually mature and also less costly to insure. Depending on the state in which you work, you may need at least one special license to operate commercial vehicles—and, of course, you'll need a driver's license.

Outlook
If you look in the Yellow Pages, you'll find a long list of limousine services. Business and leisure use of limousines continues to expand, and so do the driving jobs. Salaries and job satisfaction can vary greatly, though, depending upon the size of the city in which you work and quality of the company that employs you.

driver must be concerned if there's another car alongside traveling at the same speed. Why? Because motorists and their passengers tend to gawk and point at limousines, and your passengers expect privacy. So

David Lee, limousine driver

Don't discuss religion or politics with a passenger! That's one rule of the Overland Limousine Service in Kansas City, Missouri—and you might figure that's a hard rule to obey for driver David Lee. After all, he's a minister at Guiding Star Missionary Baptist Church.

But he's careful to stick to company rules, especially because he also trains other drivers. "You have to remind yourself that your job now is not counseling, it's driving," Lee says. "You don't want to infringe on someone else's religious beliefs. Politics and religion are not to be discussed. If the client brings it up, the correct response is to be very vague. If the person's a Democrat, let them be a Democrat. If the person's a Republican, let them be a Republican. Our job is not politics or religion, but to provide the best service."

Lee has spent his adult life either conducting a service or providing one. He found the limousine business to be a natural for him because he'd worked in restaurants, retail stores, and a major downtown Kansas City hotel, before he became a driver in 1998. During more than a dozen years in the hotel business, he started parking cars and eventually was promoted to assistant manager. So Lee knows a thing or two about customer service and drills its principles into every driver he trains.

"We're seeking persons who love the service industry," he says. "All we do is give service. People come if you have the right product and service. Build it and they will come, and they will keep coming back if the service is good. If the service is poor, they're not coming back—and remember, you're not the only company in this business."

That's why Lee's training emphasizes a pleasing attitude and appearance. Overland drivers wear black suits, black shoes, and white shirts and ties. They'll sometimes wear traditional chauffeur caps for formal affairs. And while Overland will drive all kinds of passengers, it specializes in corporate clients. Because businesspeople hire cars often, they're usually quick to spot substandard service. "They're going to notice the condition of the vehicle and the demeanor of the driver," Lee says. "Is he happy in what he's doing and is he friendly? They'll also notice his dress—is he professional? What about our track record? Are we always on time?"

Yet there are times when it's the driver who has to worry about the demeanor of his client. Drivers may be transporting teenagers on prom nights or adults who go bar hopping. Lee trains drivers to be tolerant, yet vigilant. "The driver always has to be in charge," he says. If it's for a prom, a graduation, a birthday or a bachelor or bachelorette party, the driver has to make sure they follow the rules, but also let them enjoy themselves. "For a prom, we make sure they have sodas, water, and other legal things," he says. "But we have to be mindful of illegal things slipping into the vehicle. You offer them control of the stereo system. That takes you away from being the mean driver to the friendly driver. You also have a contact number for whoever booked the party or a parent. If something goes wrong, we know to get hold of that parent."

Any driver sooner or later will wind up with an intoxicated passenger. "You try to be as close a friend as you can without going overboard," Lee says. "You have to communicate and assure them you'll take care of them. If it gets to a certain point, you move them toward their home. If it goes beyond their self-control, you may deal with the authorities. It all goes back to the professionalism of our drivers."

if you're a limousine driver, you'll try to avoid driving alongside cars right next to you. That's just one of many fine points on which you'll be trained.

As a limo driver, you'll follow a detailed set of rules and procedures aimed at giving your clients good service, safety, and comfort.

Your dispatcher will tell you the night before which calls you're scheduled to make the next day. Before your first pickup, you'll make sure your car's interior and exterior is clean and sanitary. You'll have local and national newspapers neatly folded on the back seat, and you'll stock the car with bottled water, mints, champagne, soda, and any other refreshments that are popular with passengers. Most companies will expect you to wear a suit, black shoes, and a white shirt and tie.

If your first pickup is scheduled for 6:30 a.m., you'll call your dispatcher to say you're on the way. You'll try to arrive at 6:15 a.m. to give the client the comfort of knowing the car's waiting. If you're at a private home or apartment, you won't ring the doorbell because someone in the household may be sleeping. As soon as the client appears, you'll meet him or her, take any luggage, and put it in the trunk. You'll open the back passenger door (although the client is welcome to sit up front). You'll then head for your destination and inform your dispatcher that you've picked up your passenger. Along the way, you'll drive safely and smoothly, avoiding abrupt stops and starts. If your client has a cup of coffee, you don't want it spilling on an expensive business suit.

You won't get into a conversation unless the client starts one. He or she may not be in the mood to chat or may be preoccupied with business or personal matters. You need to be sensitive to the client's needs without becoming a nuisance. For example, if you notice the client looking for a pen, you'll take a pen you have for just this situation and hand it back while you still look straight ahead. If there's a wreck ahead or an unexpected detour, you'll take an alternate route, because you'll be expected to know your city like the back of your hand. If you're dropping off your passenger at the airport, you'll call ahead to verify that you're headed for the correct terminal. And you'll unlock the doors before you come to a stop. Why? Because passengers usually try to open their door as soon as the car stops and you don't want them fighting the door handle. If the client isn't yet out of the car, you'll open the passenger door. Then you'll get out the luggage and collect payment. (Your pre-pickup instructions will tell you if the client pays you or gets billed.) And you'll always thank the passenger for using your company.

All depending upon your customer's request or needs, you could be driving a limousine or town car, which is a smaller luxury vehicle. Or if a family of five is going to the airport with a lot of luggage, a van or SUV may be needed. If you're transporting a youth baseball team, you might drive a bus.

You might need special licenses to drive some or all of these vehicles. Some states require a chauffeur's license to drive a limousine or town car while other states require only a standard driver's license. Some states may require special licenses to transport groups of 15 or more. But there is no license for the most important requirement—the ability to make clients feel that you've cheerfully provided them a service that was definitely worth paying for.

Pitfalls

You'll find yourself scrambling when a client's incoming flight is delayed or you need to make a pickup on short notice. You'll have to find time for regular exercise because you can get out of shape sitting all day and eating at irregular hours. You might catch colds and other illnesses from passengers, and you'll experience the normal frustrations and hassles of everyday driving—all day long.

Perks

You'll meet interesting people from all walks of life, and you won't be tied down to a desk. You can make a pretty good income, even if you lack a college education.

Get a Jump on the Job

When you learn to drive, pay special detail to driving smoothly and safely and knowing the rules of the road. If you can work part time in any service business, such as a restaurant or retail store, you'll start learning how to make each customer feel special.

MAGICIAN

OVERVIEW

Is your hand quicker than an audience's eye? Would you enjoy performing tricks that will brighten a child's eyes or astonish any adult? If so, there could be magic in your future.

Magicians don't really need the world's quickest hands or craftiest minds, but they must have an entertainer's flair. Of course, one of the best parts about making magic is that you're not usually playing to a tough crowd: The audience is almost always receptive—they *want* to be fooled and entertained. They want to laugh and gasp. Most of all, they want to pretend that magic is real.

Few other forms of entertainment captivate as many people of all ages as magic. The pioneer of prestidigitators, or those who practice sleight of hand, was Jean Eugene Robert-Houdin, who performed in Paris during the 1840s. His name and legacy were honored by Erich Weiss, who, as "Harry Houdini," became internationally known for astonishing escape tricks and fabulous entertainment. Houdini's showmanship taught other magicians the value of establishing great stage presence and rapport with their audience.

Houdini's followers, such as David Blaine and David Copperfield, command worldwide tours and network TV appearances that bring in millions of dollars annually. Houdini also blazed a path for lesser magicians who make a good living working on cruise ships and at major resorts. And let's not forget the local magicians who work at birthday parties, restaurants, hotel lounges, picnics, and trade shows.

The real magic lies in getting started. For a beginning magician, a library or bookstore is a good place to start. Although magicians seldom reveal their best illusions, you can easily find basic "how-tos" for tricks for beginners. Plenty of books can teach you how to make a quarter "disappear" from one hand and "reappear" in another. Lots of good card tricks are open secrets, too. For more difficult tricks, you'll have to buy the necessary props from your local magic store.

Magicians often refer to coin and card tricks as "parlor magic," and the more sophisticated tricks as "illusions"—but all

Philip Murad, magician

The transformation of Philip Murad was truly magical. While he was growing up in Montreal, he was a shy grade-school student with poor grades. That was before Murad got excited about becoming a ventriloquist. His brother bought Philip a puppet, which became his first dummy, and that kicked off a career that soon included magic.

"That brought out a whole different persona I had that had been hiding," Murad recalls. He became an entertainer when he was eight or nine, and his grades even improved because magic gave him an incredible gift—self-confidence. "Suddenly, I was loved by millions—meaning my whole elementary school," he says. "I felt on top of the world and it gave me the confidence to do anything. But then I needed material so that I could amaze people. I picked up magic and became a professional magician and ventriloquist."

By the time he was 13, Murad was performing at as many as four birthday parties a weekend. He earned $50 a party and refined his act by spending all his earnings at a magic store. "The props are very expensive, but they do a lot for you," Murad says. "You become hooked on them. It's what you love to do and if you find a prop that amazes them [the audience], you have to buy it." One of his early props was a magic coloring book, in which brilliant colors burst forth once he says a magic word.

"I was primarily a children's entertainer," says Murad, who also practiced his ventriloquist's act with his dummy, Henry. "Then I started working in hotels and restaurants on weekends in Montreal, and that helped promote me as a local entertainer."

Billed as the Philip and Henry Show, he started getting regular contracts as more and more people called him for shows. "Before you know it, I was paying my way through McGill University," he says. However, Murad didn't consider magic a career for an adult, and so he majored in film and communication. Although he was still getting paid well for magic shows, he felt obligated to search for a more "serious" pursuit, such as being a doctor or an accountant.

"I didn't know any better," he says, laughing. "I got out in the real world and got a real job, for about six months. I was selling clothing for a children's manufacturer." Then he returned to the magic business with a full appreciation of the income and fun. "I didn't realize it was so great," he says. "I was one of the busiest entertainers in Montreal. Then I moved to Toronto, a bigger city where I could make a lot more money. I wound up really doing great."

Murad realized early in his career that he needed to connect with his audience. "What really makes a magician is being a phenomenal entertainer," he says. "There are a lot of people who love magic, but just do it for themselves. These people, realistically, aren't going to make a good living if they're not able to communicate with and entertain an audience. If someone is a great entertainer, he'll make a phenomenal living. If you take someone who loves magic but isn't a good entertainer, there's nothing I can do for that person."

Specific skills aren't nearly as important as an entertainment spirit, he believes, although dexterity helps. "It's work, but you can do it if you're dedicated," he says.

Eventually, Murad left the stage to start a talent agency for magicians, and now maintains offices near Buffalo (New York) and Toronto. He and his staff screen prospective magicians, train them, and book their acts throughout North America. "A lot of them fully rely on us to make a living," Murad says. "They don't want to do the marketing, scheduling, and contract work."

Although Murad no longer performs, he hasn't forgotten where he came from, nor his original partner. His agency is named Philip and Henry Productions.

tricks can be considered illusions because they give the impression that a trick is being performed magically rather than by the magician's props and skill.

There are seven kinds of illusions. When a magician seems to produce something out of thin air (such as a rabbit out of a hat), that's called a *production*. When you make something disappear into thin air, that's a *vanish*, and changing an object into something else is a *transformation*. Sawing a woman in half and making her whole again is a *restoration*, and moving an object from the stage to the back of the audience is a *teleportation*. When a person or object seems to float in air, that's *levitation*, and *penetration* occurs when a steel ring seems to pass through another steel ring.

Many of these tricks are old standbys, but the top magicians have to come up with new tricks to make them stand out from the rest. Copperfield, for instance, will spend years preparing a new illusion. He has vanished the Statue of Liberty and an airplane surrounded by spectators. He's walked *through* the Great Wall of China. He has made audience members disappear and reappear in unexpected places.

Blaine, who started out as a street magician, has performed feats of amazing perseverance. He had himself sealed for 44 days inside a transparent case that was suspended 30 feet in the air, and he claimed to receive no food. He also spent nearly 62 hours inside a closet of ice.

How do magicians perform such astonishing tricks? They usually won't say. Star magicians would lose their stature if everybody understood their tricks. And many magicians suggest that revealing their secrets could ruin an audience's fun, as well as damage the mystique of all magicians. Yet many magic secrets are sold through videos and other instructional materials. Despite this, none of these revelations seem to hurt the public's love of magic. People want to believe in magic, and if you're a good enough magician, you'll make them believe in it even more.

Pitfalls

Prepare to give up your evenings and weekends if you want regular work. You'll have to hustle and work hard if you're going to perform at several parties or other magic shows on a weekend.

Perks

You can make a good living for a long time doing something you enjoy. Audiences are almost always receptive and enthusiastic. Learning to perform magic helps youngsters develop confidence and self-esteem.

Get a Jump on the Job

You can start learning magic as soon as you're old enough to read a book and hold a coin or deck of cards. There are literally hundreds of tricks anyone can master if he or she has enough patience and enthusiasm. Perform tricks for your friends. Hold a magic show at a friend's or relative's birthday party. Even if the tricks aren't performed perfectly, you'll get applause, and you'll understand why everybody loves a magic show.

MINIATURE GOLF COURSE OWNER

OVERVIEW

Other forms of entertainment have come and gone, but from the Manhattan rooftops to the Californian deserts, Americans have been golfing their way through windmills and under grinning clown faces for more than a century. The miniature golf course is a ubiquitous cultural icon that can be found in cities, suburbs, and rural towns across the nation. And unlike other forms of entertainment, anyone can play, of any age, physical condition, or gender. It's one of the few activities that parents, kids, and grandparents can play together.

When you think of mini golf you probably picture lazily turning windmills, towering waterfalls, and mechanized obstacles. But at many courses around the country, miniature golf has evolved into a true sport played on "golf in miniature" facilities. At these modern courses, you'll find replicas of regulation golf's famous holes complete with undulations, contours, moguls, water, sand, and vegetation traps on the greens. Thus miniature golf now offers the player many of the challenges of real golf, with the added bonus of lush, botanical gardens with meandering streams and waterfalls, fountains, and realistic rock sculpturing. These newer courses provide a park-like setting for the whole family to enjoy.

Miniature golf has been a favorite of Americans since the early 1900's, when it

was actually the short game of regulation golf. The name quite frequently used in the early years was "garden golf," and it was played with a putter on real grass. Through the 1930s, bumpers started to appear on courses to keep the ball within bounds, and the playing surface changed to hard-pressed cottonseed hulls for a smoother putting surface. Americans were hooked on miniature golf as a pastime that men or women of any age could play without being a well-conditioned athlete; more than 30,000 links sprouted up around the country. There were more than 150 rooftop courses in New York City alone. Unfortunately, the stock market crash of 1929 affected courses, and the sport was reduced to "rinky-dink" golf in which players would use any space available to set up unique, crazy courses. Many courses were built under a brilliantly illuminated billboard sign with a hard sand or clay playing surface, tinted with a green dye. Obstacles were created with scavenged old tires, wagon wheels, rusty stove pipes, sewer pipes, barrels, and rain gutters. Some of these became so popular they were incorporated into courses across the country, and were the models for the obstacle-laden miniature golf today.

As the years went on, putting surfaces were standardized and today's familiar hazards or obstacles were introduced, including storybook characters, windmills, and tiny churches. In 1953, the late Don Clayton (founder of Putt-Putt Golf and Games) was a vocal advocate of miniature golf as a serious sport. Disgusted by trick shots, he designed a new and improved course that allowed only straight putting with none of the gimmicks. At the same time, other courses still featured wacky, animated, trick hazards intended to be more challenging than straight putting. These hazards required both accurately aimed shots and split-second timing to avoid spinning windmill blades, revolving statuary, and other careening obstacles.

In the mid-1980s, adventure-style courses took a page from the Disney theme parks, with exotic course names such as Pirate's Cove, Adventure Island, and Mountasia. Many were built in tourist destinations such as Myrtle Beach, South Carolina (still considered miniature golf capital of the world), with as many as 45 courses within a 20-mile radius.

Today, new courses are still being built all the time, and there's plenty of room for mini golf course owners. Half of all Americans play a game of mini golf at least once a year, on more than 15,000 courses. In 2003 alone, Americans played 502.4 million rounds of miniature golf. At an average cost of $5 per game—that's a lot of money!

Starting your own miniature golf course takes a significant amount of money—between $150,000 and $250,000 to develop an 18-hole course. The biggest chunk of that investment is in the price of land, which varies tremendously by state and region, but you don't need much. While a lot of land is nice, you can construct a course on as little as three-quarters of an acre. Despite the relatively high buy-in cost, it's relatively easy to make a profit, even in the first year of business, and it's nearly recession-proof. Even when money is tight, playing a round of mini golf is cheaper than going to the movies and often a lot more fun. On average, it costs between $5 and $7 to play 18 holes of miniature golf.

Once the course is built, one of the biggest investments is simply maintenance, which will depend a lot on the kind of course you build. The more odd bits of manmade structures you include—the more clown's mouths and windmills you have—the more painting and scrubbing you'll do. And of course, the more electrically based the obstacles, the more upkeep there will be.

The newer breed of miniature golf courses are typically built in a natural landscape, so that the only maintenance you'll do is watering, trimming, and planting flowers and plants. Most owners say that

Tom Paone, miniature golf course owner

Tom Paone was practically born on a miniature golf course, and a love of the game is in his blood. "My parents were avid miniature golfers," he says, "and as a matter of fact, the night before I was born they were playing miniature golf." Throughout his childhood, his parents always talked about owning their own course. "As time went on, we'd play a lot, and basically as the years went by I became a teacher, but I always thought [owning a mini golf course] would be a good way to supplement my income."

By 1999, Paone's parents had passed away without ever having the opportunity to make their dream come true. "I kind of built Oasis Park in tribute to them," Paone says.

After researching the business for about nine months, he and his accountant wife Andrea hired a firm and helped design their own course: Oasis Family Fun Park in Greenbush, New York, a premier 19-hole miniature golf course with an ice cream shop and bumper-boat pond complete with waterfall.

"One thing that makes it fun is I do all the landscaping on the course," Paone says. "And I grew up around pools, so I really enjoy working with the pond systems, too." Keeping the course clean and well maintained is important to him, and his customers say that's what separates Oasis Park from the competition. "We take great pride in making sure we keep everything up," he says. "We're not in a tourist area, so we're relying on repeat traffic. I've gotten to the point where I know my customers by first name, and I like that. If I start presenting a product that isn't family friendly nor safe or hygienic, then I shouldn't be doing this."

In 2004 the Paones expanded the clubhouse so customers can come inside and enjoy their ice cream, and installed the bumper boats to give customers something to do when the summer weather gets too hot and sticky to play mini golf. "A big part of our business is birthday parties, and we can keep them going all winter long," he says.

If you're interested in building and running your own miniature golf course someday, the first thing Paone advises is that you choose your builder wisely and try to find very unusual parcels of land that no one else would want. "Topography is what makes a very good miniature golf course," he says. "Various tiers, natural wooded areas where you're not being baked on a 90-degree day, and a builder that will work within those parameters." A lot of builders take a cookie-cutter approach to building miniature golf courses that Paone objects to. "You don't get just anybody to build a miniature golf course," he says. "Just because someone is really good with concrete doesn't mean they know what they're doing in building a mini golf course."

maintenance and overhead on miniature golf courses are relatively low and not too difficult. In addition to keeping the courses very clean, some owners say they change the obstacles on the runs just to keep the experience fresh for repeat customers.

The customers are key to mini golf, especially if you depend on repeat visitors. You can do everything else right, but if your players haven't had fun, they won't come back.

Pitfalls

Most mini golf courses are outdoors, which means that in many parts of the country you'll have a limited season. For example,

To start a successful mini golf course, it's important to do your homework. "Andrea and I basically went up and down the East Coast talking to owners and builders and playing courses," Paone says. "There's a lot of builders who build very nice courses, but they're not very playable. They aren't easy for a person with a stroller to get around, or for a person in a wheelchair to navigate. Granted, you may only get six wheelchairs a year, but I've got to tell you that to that person in a wheelchair, it makes a big difference."

Choosing side businesses is also important, he says. Most miniature golf courses also offer ice cream, and it's important to have a good product. "It's usually the last thing people do at your facility. If they have a good experience on your course and then they come in and the ice cream is awful, it puts a taint on the whole evening."

One of the important factors in success or failure in this business is the weather—and that's not something you can control. "We've found that if it's a 95-degree day in upstate New York and the relative humidity is 90 percent, nobody's out. It's like a ghost town." That's why the Paones installed those bumper boats. "Customers can get wet and cool off," he says. "Ice cream sales also go down the hotter it is, because people tend to not want to eat when it's hot. They tend to want to relax inside in air conditioning or sit by a pool."

Repairs are made immediately and the ponds kept algae free all summer long. "We have 5,000 [paving stones] on our course, and every week we kick every one, because if someone trips over a paver, we're seeing them in court and we'll lose because it was in disrepair." Injuries are also a part of mini golf ownership. "This year we had five children who bloodied their parents with golf clubs," Paone says. "There can be some frustrations on a course. We've had split-open heads, sprained ankles, you name it."

In the summer, Paone is at the course almost every day, and one of the biggest challenges is dealing with his customers. "We had the guy who got out of his car, ripped off his shirt, did a belly flop in the middle of the pond and then left," he said. "Another poured alcohol into the pond when we told him he couldn't drink on the course. I spent 15 years in the classroom and I thought I dealt with stupidity, but when dealing with people on a miniature golf course, it's amazing what they do. I've seen it all. Just like any other business, it has its moments," Paone says. "Whenever you're dealing with the public you're always faced with challenges, but for the most part I really enjoy it.

"I think teaching really has helped me out as a business owner because I'm constantly dealing with education of employees and the public and kids. It's a natural fit."

in most of the Northeast, courses are open for only five months of the year. You'll need to work hard to build and run a good facility to make back your initial investment in the first year. Financing also can be tricky, because banks (especially small local banks) can be skittish about lending $500,000 for a mini golf course. If the business fails, the bank would wonder what they do with the property that's left behind.

Perks

Mini golf is just plain fun—a laid-back kind of entertainment that appeals to most people. Most owners really love the sport and enjoy hanging around the course. After the initial investment, there isn't a lot of money you need to keep adding, and the income can be very high for a fairly minor amount of work.

Get a Jump on the Job

If you dream of owning a mini golf course someday, you're probably already an enthusiastic player. Visit as many different courses as you can, and play them all. This way, you'll have a much better idea what makes a good course, what players like and what they don't. But being a good player isn't going to make you a successful course owner—that takes business smarts. Start by getting a part-time job after school or in summers at a course, and take all of the business courses you can in high school and college. The more you know about running your own business, the better.

PAINTBALL PARK OPERATOR

OVERVIEW

Paintball—described sometimes as a war game and sometimes as a sport—is a child of the extreme sports generation, and is very popular among teenagers and 20-somethings who love nontraditional sports with an edge. Some 10 million players a year, armed with air guns, knock opponents out of the game by hitting them with paint-filled pellets that splatter upon impact. Players wear protective equipment and don't suffer serious injury—except to their pride. They'll also carry around some black and blue bruises to prove they've been playing paintball.

When paintball began back in 1981, it was a makeshift game played outdoors, until paintball fans and entrepreneurs gradually realized that players needed a permanent facility to practice their new passion. Today, paintball park facilities rent air guns and protective equipment, offer pro shops, and hire referees to officiate games. Although these facilities have become very popular, they often struggle to generate a lot of income. Still, the sport is in its infancy, so who knows how much it might grow?

Paintball might not exist had it not been for a forestry group that in the mid-1960s asked the Nelson Paint Company to manufacture a paint-filled ball that could be fired from an air gun, which would be used to mark hard-to-reach trees for cutting. The paint company could make the paintballs but not the guns, so the foresters approached an air gun manufacturer who

had a model that could fire paintballs. Nobody envisioned this as a sport until two friends, Charles Gaines and Hayes Noel, got into a friendly argument about which man was best equipped to survive a one-on-one gun fight in the wild. Gaines bought some air guns and paintballs, and in 1981, he and Noel staged the first known paintball game.

Since then, the air guns have become more sophisticated and use water-based paint that easily wipes off. Although the

Jackie Johnson, paintball field manager

Jackie Johnson and her husband John are college-educated entrepreneurs who could be earning a lot more in the corporate world than they do by running Jaegers Paintball Park in Kansas City, Missouri. Jackie has a degree in English from the University of Missouri-Kansas City, and John has an M.B.A. from nearby Rockhurst College. But after graduation, Jackie worked for two companies that went out of business, and John worked for a telecommunications firm that kept laying him off and rehiring him—so the couple looked for a business in which they could have better control over their jobs and lives.

The couple was among a dozen investors who opened a paintball field in 1994. "We did not 'build it and they came,' like we hoped," Jackie Johnson says. "It took us two years to get it going. The sport was pretty much underground at that point. It got real mainstream about 2000."

The Johnsons knew paintball was growing and hoped they could carve out a healthy share of the Kansas City market. They did their homework and came up with a business plan. Whenever they took vacations to Florida and California, where the sport quickly became popular, they'd visit paintball facilities. Soon, they understood how to service customers and run a sound business. "It's a business first and paintball second," says Jackie Johnson, who works about 60 hours a week as an office manager, bookkeeper, and marketing director. "We've seen a lot of people who loved the sport but failed because they didn't know the business. Any business skills you can bring are a plus."

When the Johnsons and their partners got ready to build their business, they found an unusually attractive location—an old limestone mine. It's one of several old mines that have been turned into a small complex of offices and storage facilities. The paintball facility covers an acre, with five fields belowground and three above. The low ceilings, cavernous rooms, and natural columns add a sense of adventure. It's the kind of atmosphere fit for an Indiana Jones movie. The mine is well lit and a couple of black and white cats are in charge of critter control; at 58 degrees, it provides a cool respite from brutal summer heat. Because of the unique environment, some tourists come as much for the mine as the paintball.

Jaegers Paintball Park will draw 300 customers on a busy weekend day and is host to birthday parties, bachelor parties, youth groups, and corporate team building. Some companies view paintball as a good opportunity for employees to develop teamwork while having a good time. "It's a fun job because people come in happy," Jackie Johnson says. "It's usually an occasion. I consider it a sport, not a war game. We'll draw people from 12-year-olds to 40-year-olds, men and women. We get a lot of tourists and a lot of first-timers." The facility also attracts competitive players who practice in a separate area.

Some of the competitive players work behind the counters, distributing the guns, paintballs, and protective equipment and serving as referees. One referee, Dave Latier, is a part-time employee who competes for teams at tournaments in Los Angeles, Orlando, Chicago, and other cities. Most employees at Jaegers work there mainly because they enjoy the sport and atmosphere. The pro shop manager, Glenn Schade, is a retired engineer. He sells colorful gear and jerseys, designed to highlight paintball's "extreme sport" image. The pro shop also stocks the latest tournament guns, which can fire 18 balls a second and can cost more than $1,000.

Though the Johnsons would love to see paintball really find the American mainstream, for them the sport will always be "underground."

paintballs are soft, they travel at least 200 miles an hour, and can severely injure an unprotected face.

That's why, if you manage a paintball facility, you must make sure all players are properly outfitted and sign waivers promising not to hold you responsible for death or injury. Before players take the field, you must give them a detailed presentation about paintball rules and safety precautions. Once players are shot, they must leave the field and raise their hands above their heads to let opponents know they've been shot. If you get within 10 feet of an opponent, you must allow him or her to surrender. You're required to obey the referees (usually young paintball enthusiasts). They work for minimum wage; in some facilities, all they get is practice time.

Most paintball facilities offer more than a dozen different games modeled on familiar kids' games. In the basic game, two teams shoot at each other until one team has been eliminated or has surrendered. In another game, both teams try to capture a flag in the middle of the field. Players take breaks between games to reload, adjust equipment, cool off, have a drink, and wipe their masks. The fields include barriers and other hiding places that make the games more challenging and enjoyable.

Most facilities have advanced fields for competitive players. Top paintball players belong to commercially sponsored teams that compete in tournaments for cash or prizes. A select few actually earn a living playing paintball and endorsing jerseys and equipment. But recreational players remain the bread and butter of the business. Paintball games are especially popular for birthday parties and other group outings. If you can provide groups with an enjoyable and safe time, there's a good chance that you'll see them again.

Pitfalls

You'll work long days and most evenings and weekends, which are the most popular times for paintball. Don't count on making a lot of money in this business just yet.

Perks

You'll work in a casual atmosphere and your customers almost always are pumped up to have a good time. It's a good environment for people who don't like sitting behind a desk or wearing business suits.

Get a Jump on the Job

Try playing paintball to see if you like the game and atmosphere. Most facilities will allow you to play if you're 10 or older. To become a paintball expert, become a referee. Check out the pro shop for the equipment and uniforms used by serious players.

PARADE FLOAT DESIGNER

OVERVIEW

When you think of the Rose Bowl Parade, you probably think "flowers"—but it's what's under that carpet of beautiful blossoms that really makes the whole thing come together. And the person behind the creation of these magical sculptures is the parade float designer.

Creating the giant floral masterpieces that have become the hallmark of the Rose Parade takes a lot of skill and effort. About a year before the parade, the designer sits down with a sketch pad and tries to come up with a schematic drawing to serve as a guideline when the frame of the float is built. The generators and engines that move the float are first tucked into the frame. Next, the flat surfaces of the float are covered with wood, and the curved surfaces are covered with screening and spray-on chemicals. Many of the smaller, intricate figures on the float are carved out of foam. The float designer supervises this work and creates many of the artistic renderings. Next, the entire float is painted in different colors corresponding to the flowers that will be attached, to serve as a guide for the thousands of volunteers who will be decorating the float the week before the parade.

Seeds, bark, and some greenery can be applied months ahead of time, but the flowers must all be applied at the last minute. Hardy flowers such as mums are removed from their stems and glued directly onto the float. More delicate flowers that

AT A GLANCE

Salary Range
$40,000 to $100,000

Education/Experience
A degree in art or design is helpful; experience working with flowers or working as a volunteer on float creation is a good idea.

Personal Attributes
Patience, artistic flair.

Requirements
No specific requirements.

Outlook
Fair. This is not a career with many job openings, but there will always be some jobs available.

last only a day or two, such as orchids and roses, must be inserted into individual, water-filled vials and then stuck into the foam covering the float.

The best-known float design firm, the Phoenix Decorating Company, uses 300 tons of steel to build an average of 20 to 22 floats for the annual Rose Bowl Parade. They'll also use 70,000 square feet of plywood, 225,000 square feet of chicken wire to form large areas for floral decoration, 350,000 square feet of aluminum screen, and 14 tons of plastic foam (that's used as a base to hold 700,000 water-filled plastic vials into which fragile flowers such as individual roses and orchids are inserted). But that's not all—they'll also use 8,000 gallons of glue and 16 tons of dry materials. And then there are the flowers—20 million of them, including 400,000 roses and 550,000 carnations.

Michelle Lofthouse, parade float designer

Ever since she was big enough to wield a paintbrush and staple flowers to a float, Michelle Lofthouse has been working for the Phoenix Decorating Company, one of the best parade float design companies in the business. Lofthouse's parents, brother, and sister-in-law also work for the company, along with a year-round staff of 25, in addition to seasonal workers and volunteers. Late every December, you'll find Michelle Lofthouse hard at work, hot-gluing mums onto parade floats for the annual Tournament of Roses Parade in Pasadena, California.

"Floats are a family business for us," she says. "I guess you could say I was born into it. At first my father didn't like the idea of my being a 'floatbuilder,' but I had a knack for drawing."

Lofthouse didn't start out with flowers in mind, but she started designing floats for the Phoenix Fiesta Bowl parade back in the early eighties. Then came the opportunity to design her first Rose Parade float for the City of Los Angeles for the 1985 parade. "Things just progressed from there," she says. She was 21 at the time, majoring in music but taking a couple of art courses in illustration and design.

"Most of the experience has been on the job, however," she says, "as float designing has its own unique challenges and parameters." Although she'd never really planned to be a float designer, the opportunities presented themselves. "I figured that being paid to draw was a pretty fortunate career for me!" She believes that her education in music has helped her design. "Both art forms require the use of line, flow, and even color. The media are just different."

Still, designing floats isn't just about drawing and painting. "I think the challenging parts of float design are the deadlines," Lofthouse says. "Sometimes the design just doesn't seem to 'come,' but you have to produce something because a meeting will be scheduled. In an ironic way the deadlines are helpful, too, as you don't have time to spin your wheels too much and consequently the design often has more spontaneity. Things can become 'over-worked' and end up looking stiff if you spend too much time on them."

There are extra challenges in that her job is part of a family business. "Everything is on a more personal level," she explains. "But again this can be a 'plus' for the same reason."

She's learned how to sculpt in papier-mâché and foam, and decorate the floats with flowers, fruits, vegetables, leaves, seeds, and spices.

Typically, she starts to design a new float almost a year ahead of time, seeking inspiration from paintings, art, novels, or her environment. One year, she created a float based on her family's antique silver rose, which won the Queen's Trophy for best use of roses—one of many awards Lofthouse has won as a designer. "Some favorite subjects of mine are nature and space exploration, and we've done some pretty cool animated units involving these subjects. Dinosaurs come to mind here. . . . They are great fun to animate and some really diverse material can be used to decorate the scaly surfaces."

Most years, in fact, Phoenix builds more floats than all other builders combined. As the largest buyer of flowers for the Rose Parade, Phoenix has its pick of the best blossoms worldwide. Because of the size of its floral needs, Phoenix has its own growers to meet many of its decorating requirements.

(continues)

(continued)

If this sounds like a dream job to you, Lofthouse cautions that the realm of float-building is a very small one, and therefore tough to get into. "My advice to anyone wanting to be a part of this process would be to start at the most basic level—decoration," she says. "This is when the most people are involved in the Rose Parade Float process and where you could probably learn the most. The vast array of dry and fresh materials going on these floats is incredible. This is what the public sees when a float goes down Colorado Boulevard—the final layering.

"If you like what you see at this point and want to go further, then I'd come to one of the float-building sites and see what goes on underneath this floral covering—the sculpting, welding, and engineering that's involved. There are so many more aspects of float-building than the design. Many processes and artisans are involved in bringing a two-dimensional drawing into a three-dimensional float. I'm privileged to be at the very beginning of this process."

But the designer is just one of the people involved in building floats—it also involves the skills of an art director, animation designer, and construction coordinator, supported by the finest sculptors, construction crews, and decorators, to guarantee that every completed float is exactly what the sponsor ordered.

Pitfalls

There can be a lot of stress in this job as you struggle to come up with original, unique designs for a variety of clients, and then make sure that the ultimate float matches up to expectations.

Perks

If you've got an artistic eye and you love working with flowers, it can be an exciting experience to be involved with creating some of the country's most impressive parade decorations.

Get a Jump on the Job

Lots of volunteers are used on every float created for the biggest national parades, so you can practice your skills just about as soon as you can wield a glue gun. Also, you'll want to take as many art and design classes as you can find. You might also consider getting a part-time job in a florist shop so you can get experience working with flowers.

PARTY PLANNER

OVERVIEW

Just about anybody knows how to enjoy a party. But not everybody knows how to plan one—a need that's created a niche job: party planner.

If you enjoy being around people and love throwing parties, party planning can allow you to make a business out of an activity you once considered strictly for pleasure. Fortunately, many people initially excited about the idea of a party quickly become panicky when they are faced with all the details. This is where you, as a party planner, can come in and rescue the situation. Party planners are in greatest demand for birthday parties, weddings, bar and bat mitzvahs, corporate parties, and other social events, where they use their experience to anticipate a host's every need and problem so they can turn the event into a smashing success.

Because the planner knows how to get things done ahead of time, he or she won't get caught scrambling to take care of last-minute details. The planner will also help party givers get the most bang for their bucks. As a party planner, you'll have a good idea how much food and drink you'll need for the expected number of guests so the host won't be left with a year's worth of leftovers and a needlessly big bill. You'll also offer the host a list of party services, including entertainment.

Successful planners are as comfortable with a formal party as a casual one. If the party host wants a special theme, you can

AT A GLANCE

Salary Range
$25,000 to $75,000

Education/Experience
You don't need special training, but most party planners began by decorating cakes and planning parties long before they did it professionally. They usually organized parties for their kids and gained the experience to plan bigger and more highly organized parties.

Personal Attributes
You'll need to be outgoing and let customers know they can expect a fun time. You'll have to be patient with kids because they can easily become bored and rambunctious, and you'll have to be able to think on your feet and fix problems that might arise.

Requirements
You'll need a ton of energy, because you may work several parties in one day. You'll also need the business savvy to keep good financial records and price your services so you can get a lot of business and make a decent living.

Outlook
There will always be jobs for party planners, especially in metropolitan areas. You may not have as much luck finding clients in a small city or rural area. In a small market, you'll probably have to be the only game in town to survive.

suggest decorations and food to fit that theme. You might suggest food be served at a buffet or ordered from a menu, and advise hiring a caterer or ordering party food from a supermarket. Food stores have become big suppliers for the party business.

You should also be able to suggest a party location if the host doesn't want to hold the

Kathy O'Malley, party planner

People seldom grow up expecting to become party planners; they usually fall into the job, and Kathy O'Malley was no exception. When she got divorced, she needed a job to support herself and her children, but also wanted to stay home. "My sister suggested: 'You're good at parties, why don't you do this?' " O'Malley recalls.

O'Malley was also experienced with training horses—she'd owned ponies since she was eight years old, managed a jumping and dressage facility, and worked on a breeding farm. Ponies, she realized, could be the life of her parties. So back in 1990 she founded Cathy's Custom Parties and Ponies. (Although her first name is spelled with a "K," O'Malley knew that using "Cathy" would get her listed higher in the Yellow Pages.) "I had a pony, a truck, and a trailer," she recalls. "I could decorate cakes, I met a clown, and boom! I was in business."

O'Malley's first party pony was Sweetheart, who she bought for $125. Today Sweetheart is 47 years old and long retired, having survived a stroke and lost most of her teeth. Sweetheart and 10 party ponies spend their time outside of parties in a pasture near her Grandview, Missouri, home.

O'Malley will also provide a magician, a clown, or a moonwalk for a two- to three-hour party, making sure the entertainment doesn't clash. "The clowns want me to keep them separate from the ponies so the kids pay attention to them," O'Malley explains.

She's an extrovert who's well suited to being a host for children. "You have to be outgoing, you have to have patience," she says. "People ask a lot of strange questions. Somebody asked me, 'Do you have a pink pony?' Well, I have a strawberry roan pony and I replied, 'As a matter of fact, I do.'"

It helps to have a sense of humor, O'Malley says, and you have to be able to have fun with kids. "Kids will always cheer you up," she says. "Once in a while, I'll be grumpy and one of the kids will say something funny to pick me back up." When she was starting out, O'Malley worried about all the competition she faced. But she soon discovered, much to her surprise, that most competitors quickly left the business. "I think a lot of people are scared of hard work," O'Malley says.

She's worked as many as seven children's parties in one day. On her busiest days, she enlists her son Will, her daughter Katie, and a neighbor. O'Malley will drive around town frantically, dropping off a few ponies and a helper at one house, then go back for more ponies and take them to the next party. Although her ponies are gentle, O'Malley still carries liability insurance in case of accidents.

Ponies, unlike bigger horses, don't require much veterinary care. "The ponies are very low maintenance," she says. "They're tough and hearty. . . . My ponies are all well behaved and spoiled."

The ponies are O'Malley's trademark and keep customers coming back. "I'll hear from people who called me five or six years ago and they'll say, 'Do you still do pony rides?' " O'Malley says. "I tell them I can't afford to retire." It's doubtful she'd retire, even if she could. O'Malley would rather plan a party than a retirement any day.

party at home, such as a restaurant, country club, hall, or garden. You may need to hire a live band, disc jockey, or a string quartet.

If an event becomes big enough, such as a banquet, the host might need an event planner. Party planners handle small or medium-sized affairs, and event planners handle bigger ones.

Party planners are in big demand for children's parties, because kids usually get bored without organized entertainment. Many parents don't mind paying for a planner who can keep a house full of kids occupied for two or three hours. The hosts usually provide their own food and cake and hire the planner to bring in ponies, clowns, magicians, costume characters, rides, and games. There's usually a separate fee for each type of entertainment.

Because party planners may provide so many services, they keep a list of people and companies they can call. If a planner has four children's parties in one day, he or she may have to come up with a bunch of magicians and clowns. If a party planner gets too busy, he or she might have to hand off an entire party to another dependable planner. If a planner turns down a party, that host isn't likely to call again or recommend that planner to a friend. Party planners will get as much as half their business from repeat customers or word of mouth and the rest from advertising.

Pitfalls

Don't expect to be home much in the evening and during weekends of party season. Planning several parties at once can be stressful. Work drops off when the weather gets cold or when people are spending less, such as during a recession.

Perks

You'll be your own boss, have flexible hours, and get paid well if you have enough clients and they like your parties. You can work at home, which also can keep down your office costs.

Get a Jump on the Job

You may already be getting a jump on this job and not even know it. If you've helped plan or supervise parties for your brothers, sisters, or friends, you've already gotten a feel for this line of work. Next time you're at a block party or carnival, check out the rides and entertainers and think about which ones you'd want to hire. Check out a party shop and see what kinds of favors and other accessories are available and how much they cost.

PERSONAL TRAINER

OVERVIEW

Most Americans are self-conscious about how they look, and those who become motivated to change the way they look may go find a personal trainer. He or she is qualified to train clients to almost any level of fitness. Somebody may want to look good in a bikini as summer approaches, look good for relatives at a family reunion, or lose weight because of doctor's orders. Serious athletes may seek expert advice to move them to the next level in training, competition, or enjoyment. Even customers experienced in fitness may want a trainer to show them the newest techniques, get them motivated, or keep them company so training isn't monotonous.

A personal trainer may work full time or part time for a fitness center. Others are self-employed and may visit clients or rent space in a fitness center. You can be employed by a fitness center and visit private clients, too. Those who cater to private clients can make fabulous incomes if they train professional athletes or celebrities. Most people find a personal trainer at a fitness center and start with a consultation in which they and a trainer discuss their goals and a fitness program. These people may already be club members who pick a trainer because they've seen him or her helping others. Or they may be new members who'll want to know how a trainer might help them. If you're a trainer, you'll want to know what your clients expect to achieve and how hard they are

willing to work. You might recommend weight training, running, walking, aerobics, calisthenics, Pilates, swimming, or

Eddie Carrington, personal trainer

A few weeks before Eddie Carrington began graduate school at New York University, he and a friend walked into a Bally Total Fitness center in New York to buy a membership for the friend. Carrington, who'd developed an impressive physique while running track and dancing in college, was asked if he'd like to become a personal trainer. After the club's manager finished recruiting Carrington, his friend asked what was going on. "I told him, 'You got a membership and I got a job,' " Carrington recalls, laughing.

So he became a personal trainer in 1996 while he earned a master's degree in education. While Carrington has the academic background to teach English or French, his experience in sports and dance steered him to teaching fitness.

Bally named Carrington its national spokesperson in 2003. He attends openings of new fitness centers, has taught trendy new exercises on national television, conducts school fitness programs, and wrote a weekly column for a New York newspaper. He also trains other personal trainers, works in sales and customer service, and continues to train clients, as long as they're giving him their all. "Their level of desire is what's going to make a difference," Carrington says. "This person becomes your billboard. More than the money, you want to work with people who will put 100 percent into what you're looking to do so you can show before and after photos, or real progress. It's an hour of your time and you really want to spend that time with someone who's really into it."

One of Carrington's client cursed him as she began training. But he didn't seem to mind. "I don't mind complaining and cursing because as she's saying it, she's working hard and sweating," he says. "As long as we can see results, that's fine. I was training this one girl for a [sportaerobic] competition and she'd fight me on everything. You have people like that in the gym, too. They're purchasing your services but not putting their trust in you. It's like a relationship—if you don't trust people in a relationship, you don't want to be in that relationship. You have to trust your personal trainer and let them steer you. Some trainers like to kill their clients. I don't think that's good. You have to challenge that person, but you don't want that person the next day not to be able to get out of bed or not be able to walk because they've strained their legs too hard. People have to go back to work.

"You have to be respectful. Every person comes in with a different mentality. Some people you can be a little more hard on and some you have to coddle. Some you have to take their hand and walk them through everything, and some people take the information and run with it. You take somebody from not being able to do a push-up to doing 10 push-ups and see them get up and say, 'Yeah!' That's wonderful. It makes you feel so much better seeing how much better they feel about themselves. Or they'll say, 'I went home to visit and people couldn't believe how good I looked.' You have to tap into what motivates people."

Carrington is also a trainer, choreographer, and international competitor in sportaerobics. Carrington was part of a trio that in 2002 won the national championship and ranked fourth in the world. He somehow finds time to keep reading about the latest techniques in fitness. "There's always something new, it's all about knowledge," Carrington said. "Unfortunately, people like to work with someone who looks the part so they can say, 'This is my personal trainer. See what he looks like!' The physical expectations they have for you are greater than in any other profession, even though they're paying for your knowledge. You can get your foot in the door based on your physique. But you retain clients based on your knowledge."

a combination of exercises. You'll need to become certified in the exercises you'll be teaching. You'll be expected to pay for your own continuing education and certifications. It may cost you as much as $5,000 to take the courses you need to get certified in Pilates, a popular aerobic exercise. Some trainers become certified in massage to increase their knowledge and income. Trainers spend a lot of time and money just to train themselves.

A client may want a trainer to supervise all workouts, or just one or two a week to make sure the program stays on course. A trainer also may offer advice on nutrition and supplements that help build muscles or help muscles recover from strain. But trainers should advise clients to check with a doctor to make sure supplements are safe for them. A popular personal trainer can get overwhelmed with clients. Some trainers see as many as a dozen a day. That requires training from early in the morning, before some clients go to work, until when the gym closes late at night. A client may pay from $40 to $100 an hour in most fitness centers, with the fee split between the trainer and fitness center. A personal trainer might prefer to go out on his or her own, but will have a tougher time finding clients. Some trainers find clients by hooking up with a club devoted to running, swimming, or some other sport.

Many trainers prefer working in a fitness center because of the availability of clients and the atmosphere. You're usually working with a friendly staff in a sociable environment. You're not running around to different locations all day. And you'll have a convenient place for your own workouts, which you should consider part of the job.

Pitfalls

Some clients may show up late, cancel appointments, or refuse to work hard. Paying for certification in fitness specialties can get expensive. You might work 16 hours on a busy day and work a lot of weekends. If you're on your own, you'll find that recruiting clients is highly competitive.

Perks

Since most trainers are fitness buffs themselves, it's a chance to turn a hobby into a satisfying and well-paid job. You'll meet all kinds of people in a friendly environment. It's extremely satisfying to see clients celebrate because they have achieved a goal.

Get a Jump on the Job

If you join a fitness center, learn to use all the exercise equipment. Observe or participate in aerobics and other group activities. If there's a personal trainer around, observe how he or she works with clients. If they're not busy, most trainers will answer your questions about their jobs. You can choose from the many books, magazines, and Web sites that are devoted to fitness.

PRIVATE PARTY DISC JOCKEY

OVERVIEW

If there's nothing you love better than grabbing a microphone and interacting with an audience while spinning records, the job of a DJ could be your dream come true. DJs remix different kinds of music at parties, clubs, weddings, birthdays, and live shows, building an ambience as they get the crowd moving. The art in this profession lies in the ability to assess the mood of the crowd, putting just the right songs together with perfect timing.

Although this job doesn't really require any formal academic qualifications, it does take quite an outgoing personality and a love and knowledge of music to be successful. Some disc jockeys specialize in one kind of music or event, while others are generalists.

In addition to spinning tunes, private party DJs can also act as a master of ceremonies (especially common at weddings), coordinating the schedule of activities and getting the party rolling smoothly. Most DJs offer thousands of songs from 1920 to current tunes, because DJs are expected to be able to fulfill any request on the spot from guests.

Pitfalls

Because of the nature of the job, private party DJs usually work evenings and weekends; some may need to travel quite a distance for a job.

Perks

If you love people, love to party, and love music—what could be better than being

the emcee at an event in which you're entertaining crowds with a smooth music selection?

Get a Jump on the Job

If you're interested in becoming a private party DJ, you should concentrate in high

Tommy Demers, private party DJ

Chosen as one of the top 10 DJs in the country in 1996/1997, Tommy Demers has been spinning records at private parties for more than 20 years. Now the president of Get Down Tonight Entertainment, which provides DJs to private parties all over New England, Demers still goes out on his own DJ jobs from time to time.

In his career, he's performed as DJ and master of ceremonies with Earth, Wind & Fire, Meatloaf, Kool and the Gang, The Gap Band, and Morris Day and The Time. At Get Down Tonight Entertainment located in southeastern New Hampshire, he represents two dozen professional DJs, musicians, and vocalists. "Several of Get Down Tonight's disc jockeys are graduates of my nationally recognized, six-month intensive DJ training program," he says. "A DJ can add elegance and fun to any event." As a full-time DJ, he's still available weeknights, weekdays, and weekends, because he says he simply loves the job—loves schmoozing with the customers and choosing the music, creating that very special ambiance. A singer and music expert in his own right, Demers still enjoys spinning others' tunes as well.

school and college on courses in English, public speaking, drama, and computers; hobbies such as music are additional assets. You can get valuable experience at campus radio or TV facilities and at commercial stations while serving as an intern. Paid or unpaid internships provide students with hands-on training and the chance to establish contacts.

PROFESSIONAL SHOPPER

OVERVIEW

Get paid to shop? It sounds too good to be true, doesn't it? After all, who would pay you to do something that a lot of people consider a treat? Yet there are many people whose lives get too hectic for them to find time to buy gifts for friends, relatives, and business associates. These may be individuals who need help buying a husband or wife a birthday gift. Or perhaps a large company needs someone to buy hundreds of Christmas gifts.

Personal and professional shopping are two separate areas. You might want to concentrate on one or explore both of them. Personal shoppers cater to individuals or families and buy just one or a few gifts at a time. Professional shoppers shop for corporations and may buy gifts in large quantities. Companies use gifts to thank customers, market products and services, and generate good will. Executives are seldom inclined to study gift catalogs and often would rather turn to a professional gift buyer. In addition to holiday gifts, a company may need gifts for social events, retirement parties, employee recognition, or conventions. And it's not just large corporations who may hire you to buy large quantities of gifts. Families may need the help of a personal shopper for weddings, anniversaries, birthday parties, and other special occasions. Hosts often like to leave souvenir gifts for their guests.

You may be surprised to learn that not all clients are millionaires. None will be paupers, but they're more likely to be very busy than very wealthy. You'll usually

AT A GLANCE

Salary Range
$25,000 to $100,000+

Education/Experience
No education needed, but experience in a retail store will help you understand the different needs of customers.

Personal Attributes
You must be a people person, because your judgment is your product and you have to gain the confidence of your clients. After all, you're asking them to let you do something for them they normally might not trust anyone else to do. Your dress and accessories should be stylish and businesslike.

Requirements
You'll need good judgment to pick items appropriate in style and price for your client, and you must be familiar with a wide range of gifts and the best places to buy them.

Outlook
Because people have less and less free time on their hands, they'll need more and more help with chores such as shopping. With billions already being spent on corporate gifts, opportunities for personal and professional shoppers should multiply.

meet with a client to agree on the type of gift and price range he or she has in mind. The client may ask to see samples, tell you what to buy, or trust your judgment. In addition to paying for the gift, clients will be charged a fee based on the gift's price or the time needed to buy it. You'll look for the highest-quality gifts at the best prices. As a professional shopper, you'll have some advantages that your clients don't. You'll be allowed to pay wholesale prices at trade shows, merchandise marts, and other industry sales events. Trade shows

Emily Lumpkin, personal shopper

Emily Lumpkin wrote the book on personal and professional shopping—literally. After a successful career in this field beginning in the 1980s, she wrote *Get Paid to Shop: Be a Personal Shopper for Corporate America*. Lumpkin's success also led to speaking engagements, product endorsements, and an invitation to teach a course on personal shopping as a home-based business.

"Personal shopping is on the rise because we are all time-strapped and need help coordinating our lives," Lumpkin says. "Anyone and everyone who needs to buy a gift is a potential client. That can be the largest corporation in the U.S., a small family-owned company in your area, or your next-door neighbor." Professional shoppers must determine whether or not they want to create a large- or small-scale business and how much time and energy they are willing to commit, she explains. That will determine their path as a full-time or part-time professional shopper.

Lumpkin wanted to get back into the workplace once she'd finished raising her children, but faced a difficult transition. "My skills were as outdated as my self-confidence," she recalls. "I wondered what I could do to regain my independence, make money, and earn professional recognition. In short, what was I good at?" She had lots of ideas, but she came up with two: shopping and managerial skills. "I decided to try [personal shopping], and my business was launched," she says. "I started on a small scale, shopping for one gift designated by one client, usually for someone's spouse, uncle, or mother." Once Lumpkin got the hang of her new job, she moved into corporate gift buying. She recognized that executives often were too busy to buy gifts for customers and were happy to hire an outside expert.

"I quickly realized," she says, "that large-quantity corporate gifts resulted in less hassle, due to no returns; less pressure, due to lack of corporate involvement; and more money, due to the fact that you're buying a large quantity of the same gifts from one source, all for one client. That extended my business from personal shopping to more of corporate shopping. That involved event planning—premium buying for events that occur throughout the business calendar year, whether they be incentives for employees, thank-you's for clients, or simply marketing for company credibility." Most companies budget for such gifts, but many don't have employees in their company assigned to buy them. An outsider can relieve a company of the burden of these gift-giving events throughout the year.

Lumpkin has bought clients items as personal as an engagement ring and as risky as gag gifts. She didn't always pick the right ones. "One of my first clients had me buy 100 corporate gifts and says, 'Oh, by the way, buy a gift for my 'sophisticated wife.' " Lumpkin recalls. The problem was, Lumpkin's idea of "sophisticated" wasn't the same as the wife's. "What a mess!" she laughs. "But all business experiences will teach us many things if we let them. It's best to be open to them, affirm that you don't know everything—even if you made the business up—and learn from mistakes, strive for success, and always have integrity, honesty, and a sense of humor."

Lumpkin, who now runs Forte Publishing (http://www.fortepublishing.com) in Columbia, South Carolina, continues to recommend personal shopping to those who want to start their own business. But she cautions that personal shopping, like any other job, presents its share of problems. "Very few jobs are dream jobs," she says. "It was a fun profession. It had its many rewards and, like all businesses, had its headaches. It was a dream job in that it was mine. I was in control. If I made money, that was good for me, and if I didn't, shame on me. I was suddenly a respected professional in the community and insofar as that was a dream—yes."

will allow you to find the most up-to-date and unusual gifts. And what gift recipient doesn't like to be among the first in town to own the trendiest new item?

But it takes a special knack to make what could be a highly personal decision for your client. Picking a gift for someone else is a bit like finding him or her a date, and you won't always make the right choice. A client may not approve of the gift you bought and ask you to return or replace it. Finding clients, meeting with clients, and acquiring gifts can eat up a lot of time. Because you're helping busy people, they may not be able to contact you until an odd and inconvenient hour. If you want a more structured schedule, you could become an employee of an upscale department or specialty store and give customers fashion tips and help them pick out items.

As a paid shopper, you'll have only one chance to make a first impression. A client happy with your choices is likely to call you again and recommend you to friends or business associates. Unhappy clients are likely to find another shopper or do their own shopping. But if you have a knack for personal shopping, you'll have enough satisfied customers so that you can buy whatever you like the next time you go shopping for yourself.

Pitfalls

Long hours and finicky clients can make the job difficult. You'll probably struggle to drum up business at first. And you'll face the same risks and stress experienced by most self-employed people.

Perks

You're getting paid to do something others gladly pay to do. You can work at home, which can be a big plus. You can perform this service part time to supplement your income, and you'll meet a wide variety of people.

Get a Jump on the Job

If you like to shop, just do what comes naturally. Pay special attention to clothes and jewelry your friends and relatives buy for themselves and others. Check out stores and catalogs that sell popular gift items. Learn the art of gift wrapping. Some people are almost as impressed by beautiful wrapping as they are by a beautiful gift.

PSYCHIC

OVERVIEW

When the phone rings, do you know who's on the other end? Have you ever been *sure* you knew what someone was going to say or do next? Did you ever get a glimpse of a shadowy figure out of the corner of your eye? Most people have some degree of intuitive skill, but some believe they have more than most.

That doesn't mean that every person who is deeply intuitive feels comfortable about making it a life's work. Many worry that others will ridicule their career, or don't want to have to deal with the widespread stereotype of psychics as turbaned gypsy-skirted con artists more eager to part clients from their money than deliver an accurate "reading." Psychic counselors don't have neon signs in their windows, don't dress up in costumes, and don't charge higher fees for shady services. Psychic counselors look just like everybody else, and typically work from a deep committed sense of ethics and honor.

Psychics come in different forms: there are *clairvoyants*—those who perceive through visual means; *clairaudients*—those who perceive via auditory methods; and *clairsentients*—those who get impressions through touch, by holding an object. Still others use some mixture of different forms, including symbol systems to help focus awareness, such as astrology, tea leaves, Tarot cards, and I-Ching.

Clients typically visit a psychic when they're at a crossroads, and they need help deciding which path to travel. Some others are just curious, and want to know what events, opportunities, or obstacles are coming up. Most psychics, who offer 30-minute or hour-long sessions, record the reading so that the client has a record of what transpired. Many psychic counselors will not reschedule clients more than once a year or every six months, so the client doesn't start relying too much on readings instead of living his or her own life.

Pitfalls

Working as a professional psychic can be extremely exhausting and draining, much the way that a mental health counselor sometimes "burns out." It also involves running your own business, so you need to be good at marketing yourself to a world that may not be very accepting of your abilities.

AT A GLANCE

Salary Range

$50 to $100 an hour.

Education/Experience

Being a psychic counselor does not require formal training, although most counselors spend years studying metaphysics, meditation, and the psychic field.

Personal Attributes

Sensitivity, ability to relate to clients, good business sense.

Requirements

Psychic intuitive ability.

Outlook

Good. A skilled psychic typically has a continual supply of clients.

Victoria Laurie, psychic futurist

Professional police psychic and successful mystery author Victoria Laurie has been an intuitive for most of her life. "I first really became aware of my abilities when I was in the seventh grade," she says, "and it only took me a mere 20 years or so to come to grips with it and turn it into a profession!" Today, she lives in Arlington, Mass., with her two dachshunds, Lilly and Toby, where she gives psychic readings for clients, helps the police, and writes a successful mystery series featuring a psychic private eye. She draws from her career as a gifted clairvoyant and psychic to create the character of Abigail Cooper, the star of her three mystery novels.

She got the idea for the mystery series because she'd been frustrated with fiction that portrayed psychics as kooks relieving the gullible of their money. "It irks me that we psychic-types have gotten such a bad rap from Hollywood, and society in general," she says. She wanted to give a more accurate perspective by creating the character of Abby Cooper, Psychic Intuitive.

"I'm madly in love with both being a writer and a psychic," she says. "I not only get to do one thing that I love for a living—I get to do two. How incredibly lucky that is! I'm in awe of where life has led me, and I'm so unbelievably grateful for these opportunities and to be someone who can't wait until tomorrow because I get to repeat it all over again. So few people get to live this way, and to be one of them is the most satisfying feeling in the world. I'm truly blessed.

"Psychics are really normal people," she says. "We simply have a heightened sense of awareness." What psychics don't do are go into trances, faint at the drop of a hat, or cast spells on people they don't like, she says. "We're simply able to glean little hints of things to come, and this is where we can truly come in handy!

"I tell people who are hesitant about going to a psychic this: If you had some sort of satellite gizmo on your dashboard that could tell you there was a boulder in the road up ahead, wouldn't you want to glance at it? That's truly all we do. . . . we just let you know when to speed up (opportunity coming!) when to slow down (traffic jam ahead!), and when it might be prudent to take a different path altogether (short cut—this way!). There's truly nothing to fear."

Of course, the life of a psychic isn't always easy. "People can be insensitive because they don't understand intuition," she says. "The best thing you can do is explain to them how it works for you, and take the fear right out of it. There is a huge part of me that wishes people were more open-minded, but I think that very slowly with shows like *Medium* and books like mine, people are starting to come around. I've actually been more surprised by how accepting people have become rather than how suspicious I think they're going to be."

Laurie explains that she didn't set out with the intention of making a living as a psychic. "For me the whole thing occurred as a dare," she laughs. Laurie was trying to convince a friend of hers who was a budding psychic medium to turn professional. "All of a sudden she says: 'I will if you will,' and put me on the spot!" Laurie says. Thinking there was no way her friend would ever go through with it, Laurie took the bet. "And wouldn't you know it?" she says. "She called my bluff! But looking back, I'm so happy I was pushed by my friend. It was one of the greatest gifts I've ever gotten."

Intuition is a natural ability that everyone has to some degree, she says. "My advice to kids with this ability is not to fear it and to understand that these types of abilities aren't happening to you, they're happening for you," she says. "You are in complete control, even though it doesn't always feel that way." She suggests that anyone interested in figuring out if they have any psychic ability visit

(continues)

(continued)

this Web site: http://www.gotpsi.com. "If you want to develop it, there are lots of safe ways to try," she says. "There are a few good books out there, Laura Day's *Practical Intuition* being at the top of my list. There is nothing to fear."

Above all, don't take yourself too seriously. "Intuition is a tricky thing," she says. "We can all be wrong because there's so much interpretation going on. Keep it light, and fun and casual and you'll do well. Every one of my readings has something to laugh about. Use humor; it will serve you well."

But it's not easy to make a living at being a full-time psychic. "The way you get there is by practice, practice, practice," she says. "I'm still improving. With every reading I get better and better. I never wanted to do this if I couldn't be awesome at it, and I raise my own bar every day.

"There is no greater thrill for me than giving someone hope," she says. "Most people who come to me come because they are afraid of the situation they're in. We all go through rough times, after all. So when I can tell a client that I see things getting better, and how to make that happen—it's just the most wonderful feeling. You can hear it in their voice at the end of the session, they've stopped being afraid, and they can move through the fear on to the 'what to do about it' stage. They are empowered to take back control of their life, because they know what opportunities wait for them."

She remembers reading for one young man when she suddenly blurted out: *Why are you thinking of driving your car into a tree?* "His mouth fell open and his eyes told me I'd hit it right on the mark," she says. "He'd been having thoughts of suicide. I talked with him for a good hour after that, about how suicide was the worst thing you could possibly do because it meant that your soul would have to come back and repeat this life all over again with similar parents, choices, and circumstances. I remember saying: 'You've made it this far, kiddo, 18 years you've come through already. And if it's been as rough as you say it has, why would you want to repeat that all over again?'" Laurie discovered that he'd been so shaken by their discussion that he'd decided never to consider suicide again. "He made it through that rough patch, and went on to study engineering in college with a bright future for him."

There have been many others like this—women who were trapped in marriages with abusive husbands who just needed to see they could get out of these terrible circumstances. Others who had been putting off surgery because they were afraid of the outcome, and who were able to set aside those fears and get healed because Laurie saw them having an end to their pain. "This job is so rewarding in that way," she says. "Fear can stop you cold. It can limit your progress, prevent you from moving on to a better life, and make you do things that aren't in your best interest. If I can remove that for people, and show them how brave and strong they really are, then I've done a good day's work."

Perks

Most professional psychics get into the business because they truly want to help others, and they get enormous pleasure out of working with their clients and listening to their problems.

Get a Jump on the Job

Do lots of reading in the field to see if this is something that interests you and to see if you have intuitive gifts.

RENAISSANCE FESTIVAL PERFORMER

OVERVIEW

Do you enjoy dressing like an actor or actress in a Shakespearean play and addressing nobles as "milord" and "milady"? Do you enjoy watching armored knights jousting? Are you captivated by jugglers, storytellers, musicians, pirates, and other rogues from 16th-century England? If you sometimes wish you could have lived during this historic period and you like to perform, you'll feel right at home as a performer in one of the many weekend Renaissance festivals held each year throughout the United States. These festivals celebrate the late stages of the Renaissance, which actually began in the 14th century and marked the transition from medieval to modern times.

Performers are paid but they also pass the hat for tips. Some make a living by traveling the fair circuit throughout spring, summer, and fall. John Mallory, a festival fixture, throws knives at family members. These dedicated performers usually boost their income by selling personalized T-shirts or video discs of their shows. These entertainers earn every penny because they routinely perform four shows a day.

If you've performed in Shakespearean plays, you're already familiar with the speech, dress, music, and humor of that era. You might adapt what you've seen in those plays and create a musical or comedy act. You could learn how to walk on

stilts or become a street juggler of Indian pins, knives, or fire.

Once you've developed an act, it's time to audition. If there's no fair near you, you can send an audition tape to a festival in which you'd like to perform. If you have experience at another Renaissance festival, you might ask the director there to give you a recommendation.

Once you're hired, you'll have to take care of details that are important for any

Paula Strange, Renaissance festival performer

If you visit a Renaissance festival in the Midwest, you're likely to see Bess the Bard, an Irishwoman who tells children's stories, and Gypsy and the Jester, who perform such shows as "Pirates For Dummies." Bess and the Gypsy are creations of Paula Strange, who spends weekdays in the insurance business in Overland Park, Kansas, and weekends at Renaissance festivals in Bonner Springs, Kansas, Council Bluffs, Iowa, and St. Louis and Jefferson City, Missouri.

Strange started out as a festival storyteller and teamed up with Dennis Porter to create "The Gypsy and the Jester." In their show "Pirates For Dummies," the jester (Porter) announces to the gypsy (Strange) that he wants to become a pirate. So the gypsy tries to educate him. "I teach him how to look like a pirate, hunt for treasure, how to get the girl, how to sing like a pirate, and how to fight like a pirate," Strange says. "Then he has to pass a test. And I tell him he has to pass it in the middle of a raging storm, so I throw a cup of water in his face. He picks up a bucket to throw it on me and it turns out to be birdseed. We also bring people on the stage. It's extremely important to have the kids in the audience interact."

Strange was originally a theater major at Southwest Missouri State University but changed her major and received a law degree at Southern Methodist University in Dallas. She got hooked on Shakespeare when she was eight years old, and by age 14 was performing in Shakespearean plays with community theater groups.

Strange was asked to become a children's storyteller at the Renaissance festival in Bonner Springs. "I was pretty awful when I started, I was doing it right out of the book," she recalls. "Eventually, I got a style of my own. I developed the character, Bess the Bard, and took it to schools, libraries, Cub Scout troops, and churches." Bess is a lower-class Irish woman from Castle Blarney who tells Irish history stories, such as the tale of Grace O'Malley, the pirate who convinced Queen Elizabeth I to have O'Malley's sons and brother freed from jail.

Strange performs storytelling and Gypsy and the Jester during eight shows a day. "The most difficult thing for me was asking for money, because I always performed for the love of performing," she says. "You have to find a fun way to ask so you're not chasing them away and you're making them want to give. So I tell the pirate that we'd rather not plunder anymore, but that 'There are those pirate guild dues. These look like prosperous people and if they give the loot to us now, we won't have to rob them later.' "

Strange has no trouble getting into a Renaissance mood because she's an admirer of that period. "It was a time of such incredible change and helped build a lot of our modern institutions," she says. "People started thinking for themselves rather than letting the church tell them what to think. They rediscovered science from the times of the Greeks and Romans. And it was a time of really strong women, like Mary Queen of Scots. Some of Henry's [six] wives were intelligent people in their own right. It was a fascinating time and what especially interested me was Shakespeare's love of language. Wittiness and cleverness of language were prized."

Strange's husband, Michael, is a photographer and helps her with publicity for her festival shows. Their daughter Jade volunteers to dress as a princess at the Bonner Springs festival. "I have to kneel and address her as 'Your Highness,' " Strange says, smiling. "And she says, very regally, 'You may rise.' "

entertainer, making sure that your act does not violate any copyrights.

You must learn to appeal for tips, a major income source for festival performers. Your show must be entertaining enough to make the audience stay until the end. Then you need to pass the hat in a cheerful way while letting the crowd know that tips are vital to your income. A performer's day starts with a cast meeting nearly an hour before the gates open. Festivals usually open with a royal procession, and the shows start 30 minutes later. A performer's four shows are spaced out over the day and he or she is likely to remain at the festival until shortly before closing.

Some performers who work the fair circuit buy a mobile home for transportation and lodging.

Pitfalls

This is usually a labor of love—not well-paid work. Because you're self-employed rather than an employee of the fair, you'll need to buy workman's compensation insurance in case you're injured, and you'll need liability insurance in case your act injures someone else. You'll also have to pay for your own travel, food, lodging, costumes, stage props, and publicity, and you'll need to keep records of your income

and expenses when it's time to pay your income taxes. You'll always work weekends, and if you work the festival circuit, you'll be on the road traveling from one festival to the next. You'll have the same risks and overhead of any self-employed entertainer.

Perks

If you love the Renaissance and Shakespeare, independence, and interacting with an audience, there can be enormous joy in this kind of work. You'll be part of a festive atmosphere and you can become a professional entertainer without giving up your day job. Audiences are usually young and enthusiastic, and you can meet all kinds of interesting people.

Get a Jump on the Job

Even preteens can volunteer to wear costumes, run errands, or fill other roles at a Renaissance festival. Visit one in your area and check out the costumes, performances, and atmosphere. Get involved in music and theater. Read about England in the 16th century and the Renaissance in general, and attend Shakespearean plays whenever possible. You could join your local chapter of the Society for Creative Anachronism, which studies and celebrates this period.

RINGMASTER

OVERVIEW

When the circus curtain rises, all eyes are on the ringmaster—the master of ceremonies and the common thread for all the wonderful and dangerous acts to follow. The ringmaster announces, sings, dances, keeps the crowd energized, and infuses the show with vitality. This requires an unusual combination of talents, and casting directors search the entire country for candidates.

Circuses are looking not only for an impressive resume, but special qualities that enhance a show's flavor. Ringmasters set the tone as they come out to greet the crowd while wearing a tuxedo and top hat, surrounded by elephants, dancers, clowns on stilts, and trapeze artists.

Because a circus is really an elaborate theatrical production, it shouldn't be surprising that ringmasters have theatrical backgrounds. Kevin Venardos held leading roles in touring musicals and bit parts on a soap opera before he was hired as ringmaster for Ringling Bros. and Barnum & Bailey Circus in 2001. Tyron McFarlan appeared in such musicals as *Ragtime*, *Jesus Christ Superstar*, and *Showboat* before he was hired by Ringling Bros. in 2005. Ringmasters may not risk their life, as a trapeze artist or a lion tamer does, but their job includes responsibilities that in many ways make it just as demanding.

First, the ringmaster must memorize a script, as long as 40 pages, that covers the entire show. He's expected to encourage a feel-good, energetic, and electric atmosphere among the performers and crowd. If the ringmaster smiles good-naturedly and

bounces around the floor, the performers are likely to do the same. The ringmaster is responsible for the flow of the circus and needs to keep the schedule on time. This can be a chore because the acts, especially those involving animals, don't always follow the script.

While trainers do their best to avoid using animals that seem listless or uncooperative on a particular day, the animals don't always give advance warning. When an animal refuses to perform, it's up to the ringmaster to depart from the script and ad-lib. If a performer suffers an injury, the ringmaster will try to settle down the crowd and, hopefully, be able to assure everybody

Tyron McFarlan, ringmaster

Tyron McFarlan became only the 34th man ever to announce to a circus audience, "Ladies and gentlemen, children of all ages, welcome to the Greatest Show on Earth!" McFarlan was hired by Ringling Bros. and Barnum & Bailey Circus largely because of his singing, dancing, and acting talents, but he's quite certain his military experience helped him, too.

McFarlan, a native of Columbia, South Carolina, spent 13 years in the Army National Guard and was promoted to company commander. "I'm able to rein in the focus and attention of the audience members, and that calls for a commanding presence," he says. "You're leading by example. The energy we give to the public is predicated largely on the audience and how they feed us energy. It's also my responsibility to lead the performers." McFarlan is the first one out from the curtain. "When I go out with a certain amount of energy, my performers are bound to follow and give the crowd a good show."

If he's not introducing acts, he's singing or screaming the entire time. "It's extremely challenging, vocally," he says. "I drink tons of water—no alcohol or caffeine because they dry out the vocal chords and I'm trying to maintain a healthy diet."

It's imperative that McFarlan stay alert and energized on the floor, which is no small feat, since they sometimes do three shows a day. "I'm on the floor the whole time, an hour and 50 minutes to two hours. I'm often in a dark corner, should [an accident] happen. Then I'd have to go out and perform off the cuff and let the audience know everything's going to be okay."

McFarlan was performing at a dinner playhouse in Rock Island, Illinois, when the playhouse owner told him auditions were being held for a new ringmaster. Although the application deadline had passed, an audition was arranged for McFarlan in Sarasota, Florida. His chances had improved when the early rounds of auditions failed to turn up a suitable ringmaster.

"I decided to drive down and audition, so it was then that I ran away and joined the circus," McFarlan says. "I knew that well over 40 professional Broadway actors had auditioned, so I was excited to know I was able to contend with a lot of guys like that. When I audition, I believe in displaying a certain amount of confidence," he says.

Traditionally, the ringmaster has to have a certain stature, a commanding look, and most ringmasters are relatively tall. McFarlan fit the bill at six feet, four inches, and 250 pounds. "And the circus is trying to hit home the importance of physical fitness and nutrition," he says, "especially since it's such a problem with young kids." And that's not all. McFarlan is African-American, and notes that Ringling Bros. has really started to appeal to a large number of African-Americans as well as Hispanics—and from a marketability standpoint, his ethnicity plays into that.

McFarlan, at age 34, became the 34th ringmaster and second African-American ringmaster in the first 135 years of Ringling Bros. (The first African-American, Johnathan Lee Iverson, joined the circus in 1999.)

"We've had more presidents of the United States than ringmasters," McFarlan says. "This is a prominent job that doesn't come along regularly. I'm very proud to be a ringmaster."

After graduating from the University of South Carolina with a degree in criminal justice, McFarlan earned a recording contract as a rhythm-and-blues vocalist, and eventually landed a role

(continues)

(continued)

in a local musical, *Smokey Joe's Café*. He also took acting lessons and hired an agent, which led to work in television and commercials and helped him land the job at the Illinois playhouse. That, of course, led him to the circus.

"As many times as I hear, 'You have a fantastic job,' I don't consider it a job because I have such a passion for performing," McFarlan says. "It's wonderful to be able to do something that I have such a passion for and get well compensated. I'm a firm believer in doing what you like to do. You'll always find a way to get compensated if you have the passion. So it's important to get motivated and everything else will fall into place."

that the performer isn't injured seriously. Ringmasters are also taught to be safety conscious. They'll alert someone if they notice any animals or equipment out of place on the arena floor, and they learn quickly to watch their step when there's an elephant nearby—an accidental nudge from one will send you flying.

The ringmaster's role is ever expanding. Ringmasters weren't noted for singing until Harold Ronk, a former church vocalist and opera singer, was hired by Ringling Brothers in 1957. He became known as the "singing ringmaster," and most ringmasters today are expected to sing. In addition to a few vocals, including the show's opening number, the ringmaster also will have choreographed dance routines. This means the ringmaster must be in top shape and keep fit while the show's on tour. The ringmaster also has to take care of his vocal chords, because they're often under strain.

It can take more than a month to rehearse the show, because the ringmaster must become familiar with all acts, performers, and arena layouts. This can be especially challenging for a new ringmaster,

especially one who's new to the circus. In addition to all the other responsibilities, the ringmaster is required to make a lot of promotional appearances on behalf of the circus—because the ringmaster is the most visible part of the show.

Pitfalls

You're on the road and away from home a lot. Your routine is strenuous and will exhaust your legs and voice, and you may suffer allergic reactions from all the dust and animals surrounding you.

Perks

You'll earn an excellent salary and become a celebrity. You'll get a chance to showcase your singing and dancing talents in front of big audiences throughout the country.

Get a Jump on the Job

Get involved in theater, singing, or dancing. Next time you watch a circus, pay attention to the ringmaster's dress, voice, and style. Read about the ringmaster's job in books or on Web sites, especially http://www.ringling.com.

ROLLER COASTER DESIGNER

OVERVIEW

Slowly you inch straight up the metal track, up into the clouds, until you're teetering high above the ground on the crest of the ride. You peer over the top at the twisting path below and tell yourself that, surely, roller coaster designers know what they're doing.

There are about 100 roller coaster design companies in the United States, who combine both design and engineering to develop a thrill ride. For example, Arrow Dynamics, a roller coaster design company of less than 30 people, employs electrical engineers, mechanical engineers, drafting engineers, and structural designers. After a roller coaster boom in the early 1900s, the United States boasted more than 1,500 coasters; but by the 1960s, that number had plummeted to less than 200 in the 1960s. Today, there are more than 115 theme parks in the United States, and competition means that each year the race is on to come up with something faster, newer, speedier, and scarier.

Typically, roller coasters are designed for a specific park, which orders a new ride, describing the desired features and its budget. The designer then develops a proposal for the park that includes cost, design features, and environment.

A ride can be basic, suspended, looping, or straight; it can be high or medium-high and might involve water or darkness. The surrounding landscape and the available plot influence the design decisions.

The ride may have a great view or no view at all. The ride could be long or short. The capacity of the ride is another concern—how many passengers can the ride handle at a time?

If the park accepts the proposal, the engineering designer gets to work building the track, structure, stations, and controls. The designs then get sent to the manufacturers, who build the machine. Then it gets sent to the park. It can take up to a year to build a ride, and the more complicated the design, the longer it takes to build.

Cindy Emerick Whitson, roller coaster designer

Cindy Emerick Whitson is a project engineer for Premier Rides and is now managing the service and support department for the company. With more than 10 years of experience as an engineer with her specialty in material testing, she's worked in the theme park industry since 1993 and has helped procure and install many world-class attractions. She's worked on The Manhattan Express Roller Coaster and New York-New York Hotel and Casino in Las Vegas, she says, along with the Viper Roller Coaster at Six Flags Great Adventure in New Jersey, and Speed the Ride in Las Vegas.

Whitson also has supervised the design, manufacture, installation, and testing of Premier Rides' revolutionary new wooden roller coaster trains on the world record–setting Son of Beast wood coaster at Paramount's Kings Island in Ohio. She also managed the team that added the lap-bar restraint upgrades on Premier's LIM coasters across the country. She's also a member of the Ride Safety Advisory Council for the State of Ohio and part of the Ohio Water Park Safety Committee.

Today, Whitson is in charge of service for Premier Rides. In this capacity, she works with parks on upgrading and servicing all attractions.

Pitfalls

The pressure can be intense to come up with the biggest, best, fastest, scariest, wildest ride in the country, and tight deadlines can lead to massive stress. Yet you can't give in to the pressure, because any mistakes could create serious problems.

Perks

For structural engineers with artistic flair, what could be more fun than design-ing roller coasters at theme parks? Most roller coaster designers are enthusiasts themselves.

Get a Jump on the Job

If designing wild and exciting rides is in your future, you'll need to study hard while you're still in school, focusing on math and science—especially physics.

RUNNING COACH

OVERVIEW

Running can be lonesome for those hitting empty roads early in the morning. Some runners break the monotony by listening to music, while others bring a dog. Many runners prefer training with a group, which provides companionship, safety, and extra motivation.

These groups are organized and trained by a running coach, who gives club members a highly structured and effective training routine, tailored to the race schedule in their area. It's the coach's job to distribute a binder filled with the club's running schedule, course maps, and training information. The coach may change the route each week to give members variety and help runners who live in different parts of town. The club will gather together, on weekends or weeknights, and runners usually train with others who run at the same pace. There may be one group running seven-minute miles, another running eight-minute miles, and so on. In addition to long, stamina-building runs, some groups offer speed work once or twice a week.

An effective running coach will often run with the group, often starting with the slowest runners and gradually catching up to the fastest. The coach may wait for the runners at water stops on the training course, offering encouragement and advice, and then get back to the finish in time to welcome back the group.

A group run requires a lot of preparation for a coach. On a weekend morning,

the coach gets up before daylight to mark the training course with flags and mile markers, which enables the runners to stay on course and know how far they've run. The coach also sets up stands stocked with water and sports drinks to make sure the runners don't get dehydrated.

A running coach may be able to take one day off each week during running season, but most of the week is spent preparing for the next training session and taking care of business matters. A running coach

Eladio Valdez, running coach

Eladio Valdez was a two-mile runner in high school when he began to understand that a runner's final time isn't always as important as what the runner endured to earn that time. Valdez loved running track for Bishop Ward High School in Kansas City, Kansas, and became frustrated when his performances began slipping. Eventually, he was diagnosed with exercise-induced asthma. His final high school meet was filled with frustration and agony. He couldn't breathe, was sick to his stomach, and finished last. Valdez told his coach, Gary Roland, that there was no point in him running anymore.

"You always say that if the pain outweighs the gain, you should quit," Valdez reminded his coach. Roland replied, "You're not quitting, you're adjusting. You can try road races. There are other ways to run." Valdez felt encouraged. And he felt truly touched when he learned what his coach had told the rest of the team. "After I left, he called everybody over to the bleachers and says, 'If everybody had the heart of Eladio, we would be state champions,'" Valdez says. "When I heard what he said, I went over and gave him a big hug. I learned a key lesson: you do what you can and that's more important than being fast. Your time doesn't tell you everything. The journey's more important than the destination."

Valdez's club, The Runner's Edge, in Shawnee, Kansas, includes runners of wide-ranging abilities from ages 14 to 72—those who just want to finish a 10-kilometer race as well as those training for the Boston Marathon. He also coaches race walkers. "I'm into art, not science," Valdez says, explaining his willingness to coach even slow runners. "I'm into gray areas. It's not 'My way or the highway.'" Valdez has pounded a lot of roads, however, and completed 16 marathons, including one in three hours. "The number one thing is to have done what your participants are doing," he says. "I know the highs and lows. Eighty percent of what people bring up, I've experienced."

can expect constant phone calls and e-mails between group runs; one runner may want the name of a physician to treat an injury. Another may want suggestions on how to keep up a training program during a business trip or vacation. Or a runner may have left the schedule behind.

A good running coach supports his members when they train or compete, standing near the finish line to cheer on club members and sticking around to chat with members and congratulate them for good efforts.

While a running coach can't guarantee that everybody can learn to run faster, a good coach can make sure that runners will have an enjoyable and organized training program that helps them to tackle their goals. For many runners, that can mean qualifying for a major marathon; for others, it may simply mean finding a more enjoyable and sociable running experience. A good running coach will help runners at all levels get what they want from the sport.

Pitfalls

Like any entrepreneur, a running coach must always worry about keeping up club membership and income, and always be at the mercy of the weather.

His favorite part of coaching is talking to people. "You like to see the light bulb coming on—the 'aha!' moment—but it doesn't happen often," he says. "Seeing improvement, that's exciting. Knowledge is important, but being able to connect with people is even more important."

Valdez has about 300 members and offers four-month training courses in the spring and fall and a shorter winter session. He offers group runs on Saturdays and speed work during the week. He never envisioned this club getting so big when he started in 1997. Members tease him because he still crams all his equipment for group runs in the same subcompact car he drove when all he needed was one container of Gatorade.

After receiving degrees in exercise science and general science at the University of Kansas, and taking courses in nutrition at John Bastyr College in Seattle, he went back home to become a high school teacher and track and cross country coach, but decided he wasn't cut out to teach. Instead, he took a job in a running store, where owner Gary Gribble helped Valdez start a club. It eventually turned into The Runner's Edge, and Valdez quickly discovered how much he didn't know about running a club.

"A lot of disastrous things happened," he says. "For the first run, I didn't realize how many people were incompetent at reading maps. So for the next run, I gave them oral directions. That didn't work, either. For the third run, I put flags on the course." Some problems never disappear, though. Valdez always has runners who are frustrated by disappointing times. "I don't want any of them to get too down on themselves," he says. "I tell them, 'It's not a goal, it's a dream. And how often do you realize your dreams?' "

Yet, by making a living in the sport he loves, Valdez has realized his.

Perks

Running coaches are among the lucky few who can turn their hobby into an occupation. It'll give you a lot of satisfaction to see a runner's spirits lifted because he or she has recorded a personal best time or realized a goal that once seemed impossible.

Get a Jump on the Job

Start running and keep running. Most road races have children's divisions, although even grade school runners can race against adults. Join a track or cross-country club or team. Become a race volunteer at the finish line or a water station. Read running magazines and Web sites to learn the finer points of competing and coaching.

SCI-FI CONVENTION PLANNER

OVERVIEW

Science fiction conventions seemed destined to flame out quickly when they first started in the mid-1970s, since they were centered around *Star Trek* and fans who didn't want to let go of their beloved TV show. At the time, the "Trekkies" began attending conventions where they could meet cast members, get their autographs, buy mementos, and express their devotion. Many conventioneers showed up with homemade *Star Trek* outfits and props that looked more authentic than those actually on the series. Some fans built a full-sized replica of the Enterprise bridge and shipped it to *Star Trek* conventions around the nation. Three decades later, these conventions are still going strong. Cast members of classic TV series such as *Star Trek*, *Lost in Space*, and *Battlestar Galactica* are in constant demand for appearances throughout the United States and overseas.

And they don't show any signs of fizzling out. Indeed, these conventions keep growing in popularity and sophistication. In today's era of entertainment extravaganzas, no show can succeed without dazzling its customers, and sci-fi conventions are no exception. Science fiction, in fact, has become just one of the main attractions for some conventions. While there are still conventions for hard-core Trekkies, many fans attend multi-media, popular arts conventions.

The annual Dragon*Con convention in Atlanta, for instance, is a four-day event over Labor Day weekend that includes about 30 different events, or "programming tracks." One recent convention included these tracks: *Buffy: The Vampire Slayer*, *Gothic Horror*, *Star Trek: TrekTrak*, *Star Wars: Matters of the Force*, *Tolkien's Middle-Earth*, *Professional Championship Wrestling*, and *Tournament & Open Gaming*. At least a dozen bands catered

Pat Henry, sci-fi convention planner

Pat Henry was concentrating on his comic book business in Atlanta when he and six other investors got together in 1986. "Some of us were comic book guys, sci-fi literature guys, or they loved sci-fi TV and *Star Trek* things," Henry recalled. "So we decided we wanted to run a show. I drew the short straw, so I run the thing." Henry is chairman of Dragon*Con, which runs a sprawling Labor Day weekend convention in Atlanta. The first convention was held in 1987 and included more attractions than any fan possibly could attend over four days. "We try to do just about everything, we try to be all things to all people," Henry says. "To create a lot of excitement, therein lies the work, and my job is to make sure all that gets coordinated. I just have to move from one category to the next. The biggest complaint we get is that there's too much to do. And I love it!"

Basically, Henry is selling entertainment. "I have the best value in the entertainment world," he says. "People step off the planet for four days. They have a ball." Although Henry admits that it was traditionally a place for geeks, "we're not geeks anymore. We're accepted. . . . We tip well and we know how to behave in public. We do have social skills. We just don't necessarily have the same social skills that everybody else does."

In addition to his army of volunteers, Henry has a paid staff to generate fresh ideas. Because there have been sci-fi conventions all over the nation for the past three decades, it's important to offer new wrinkles. Originally, Henry offered separate tracks for *Battlestar Galactica* and *Star Trek*. "Some people were coming in from the new *Battlestar* (a 2003 miniseries) and we had Richard Hatch from the old show. And the *Star Trek* people wanted to get in with the Battlestar guys and compare series in the sixties and seventies versus series in the 21st century. We have a tremendous amount of crossover. I have track directors who come up with these ideas. Most people would call them 'insane.' I would call them 'geniuses.' "

Henry says he never doubted his ability to pull off such an ambitious project. "I guess it takes a blind optimism that it's going to work," he says. "When we got together, I was thinking, 'This is cool.' It never occurred to me that failure was an option. The [other] guys who own the show have never been greedy. They never said: 'You have to produce profits.' It was: 'Let's make the show survive.'" Eventually, the show was becoming such a financial headache that Henry and his wife and business partner, Sherry, almost decided that the 2000 convention would be their last.

"I'm only half nuts," he says. "We were just beat up. We were having all kinds of problems with the convention center and the contract. We were standing on the second floor of the Hyatt, looking down at the lobby and saying, 'This isn't a business for us. This isn't a living.' At that point, the 501st Stormtroopers were coming through the lobby to escort (*Star Wars* actors) David Prowse and Jeremy Bulloch to a panel. And the crowd starts clapping—it was really spontaneous. And my wife and I look at each other and say, 'We can't quit this. What else are these people going to do on weekends?' "

to various musical tastes. There were film screening rooms, a science fiction writer's workshop, and a parade. The first parade, in 2004, featured author Janny Wurts playing pipes while the futuristic 501st Stormtroopers marched behind, followed by Klingons,

Starfleet officers, fairies, pixies, aliens, and musketeers.

By now you should be getting an idea of how much planning goes into a sci-fi convention. Dragon*Con depends on about 1,000 volunteers because it couldn't afford to pay an entire staff for such a huge event. Its full-timers include a staff of *track directors*, who dream up new ideas for old themes. Old science fiction shows are analyzed from modern and offbeat perspectives. Dragon*Con signs up hundreds of celebrity guests from the worlds of literature, film and television, comics, music, theater, and even gaming. The key to this convention is to bombard customers with entertainment and keep them busy and stimulated from morning until night.

If your show draws thousands from out of town, you'll have to make sure they can find hotel rooms. You'll have to arrange with hotels to provide rooms for your fans at special convention rates. And, of course, you'll need to rent a hall or arena to make sure you have enough space. You'll have to set up rooms for various events and autograph sessions, get celebrity guests picked up at the airport, and set up tables for various fan clubs. You'll also need to provide customer services such as van shuttles for disabled fans, sign language interpreters for fans with hearing problems, a child care agency, security, and an information desk to help fans find their way around.

You won't have much downtime. As soon as one convention ends, you'll have to start planning the next one. You'll want to get an early jump on ticket sales and organize a marketing and public relations campaign to keep your old customers and bring in new ones.

Pitfalls

These conventions, despite their popularity, often aren't big moneymakers. Many sci-fi conventions planners are fans who invest their own money and often lose it. One company went out of business despite staging more than 200 conventions in eight years. Planning takes a lot of time and energy, and even planners who can turn a profit sometimes may wonder if the money is worth all the effort.

Perks

These conventions are a great deal of fun, and you'll get a kick out of seeing so many customers having such a good time. You'll make contacts in the entertainment world. And the experience could help you move on to other promotional ventures.

Get a Jump on the Job

If you've watched any science fiction movies or TV shows, you'll have a good grasp of why these conventions are so popular. If you attend one, check out the attractions and celebrities that make these events tick. If there's a sci-fi convention in your area, sign up as a volunteer. Then you'll start to get an idea of how much work and organization goes into the planning.

SKI LIFT OPERATOR

OVERVIEW

Do you love skiing or just soaking up the atmosphere of a ski mountain in a winter wonderland? Have you recently graduated from high school or college and want to chill out, but also make some cash while you think about your next step in life? Then working on a ski lift could be just the right job for you.

Ski lift operators control ski lifts and keep an eye on the skiers who use them. They're also goodwill ambassadors, machine operators, and safety checkers rolled into one. It's their job to greet skiers as they approach the lift and make sure they have the right ticket and get on safely. Inexperienced skiers often need help, especially when they hop off the lift too early, stumble, and flop around in the snow. Lift operators are trained to be patient and cheerful, and to try to make sure that all skiers enjoy themselves. Ski lift operators also provide information about snow and weather conditions, the difficulty of different trails, and the ski area's hours.

The lift crew gets started well before the first skier, snowboarder, bobsledder, or other winter sports enthusiast. Lift operators report early in the morning, and if there's been a snowfall overnight, they'll do a lot of shoveling to keep the loading and unloading areas accessible. Although you don't have to be an Olympic weightlifter, you'd better be able to handle vigorous work, often in freezing temperatures. The lift crew also checks that all lift buttons are working properly for routine and emergency operations. Does the

lift start and stop correctly? Are the emergency triggers working? One operator must always take a trial ride to make sure that the lift is running smoothly and safely.

There's usually a lift operator stationed at the top of the hill and two at the bottom. Even when operators are helping passengers, they're close enough to the controls to stop the lift or change its speed. Veteran operators who ski well may become team leaders who help open the lifts, give the

---

AT A GLANCE

Salary Range
$8,500 to $12,000

Education/Experience
Most resorts will expect you to have a high school diploma. Most lift operators are avid skiers, but some learn to ski on the job. Others don't ski at all.

Personal Attributes
You'll have to be alert because emergencies do occur. You should enjoy dealing with the public, especially beginners who'll appreciate your friendliness and reassurance. You'll need a neat appearance and good customer service skills. You must function well at high altitudes and not fear heights.

Requirements
You'll have to be at least 18 years old and be in reasonably good condition because hard, physical work is part of the job. You'll be expected to complete a training program. You'll have to display skiing skills to work at certain trails.

Outlook
Skiing continues to be one of America's most popular winter sports, so ski lift operators should be in demand for a long time. But it's not a year-around job, so there's constant turnover creating openings. But there are also a lot of applicants.

Karyn Lacey, ski lift operations supervisor

When Karyn Lacey and a friend first drove to Vail, Colorado, the last thing she expected was a full-time job. She'd graduated from St. Michael's College in Vermont with degrees in psychology and philosophy and figured she needed a break. "I was coming out for just six months to have a good time before I got that real job—and I never left," Lacey recalls. "I had never been farther west than Pennsylvania. I was amazed at the scenery and the mountains. I enjoyed the lifestyle. It was more relaxed, as opposed to the Northeast. It was a much slower-paced lifestyle.

"I was in shock at how genuine and nice and concerned people were. My first night in town, we stopped at a gas station and asked the guy there if he knew a place to stay that was nice and reasonable. The next thing I knew, he was calling somebody who worked at the front desk of a hotel and was getting us a room. That was not something I experienced back east. And I love to go rafting, kayaking, mountain climbing, and hiking." Lacey also devotes plenty of time to skiing and other winter sports.

She started as a lift operator at Vail and after a few years began training operators at Vail and nearby Beaver Creek. Eventually, Lacey was promoted to supervisor of Beaver Creek Lift Operations. She hires an entire winter ski lift staff of 115, which is reduced to a skeleton crew in the off-season. Lacey takes care of the payroll, writes the annual budget, revises training manuals and still helps with training. Now, friends and relatives can't accuse her of wasting her college education and becoming a ski bum! Actually, they never did.

"My parents have never said anything like that to me," she says, laughing. "They have never put me in that position. I'm happy. I love my job. I've realized I'm not somebody who's meant to be in an office all day. Of my 40-hour week, I would say I spend half on the mountain and the other half in the office."

Lacey grew up on Cape Cod, Massachusetts, and her parents also had a house in New Hampshire, where she skied regularly. She went to a college in the heart of New England ski country, and she can relate to all those youngsters who apply to her for ski lift jobs. After all, she was once in their shoes! "The majority are just out of high school and college," she says. "We have a lot who just take a year off to have fun and do something different when they're done with their serious schooling and before they're tied down. We have a handful of operators who also work golf courses in the summer." Lacey hires her staff several months before ski season, and fills a third of her jobs with overseas applicants. "Some go down to Australia, where they have winter when we have summer, and work in a ski resort," she says. "They'll do two winter seasons for eight years in a row."

She notes that her overseas applicants must speak English, which is a big part of the telephone interview. "They have to be able to understand technical information and converse with our guests," she explains. Even if they don't share the same home country, Lacey's operators seem to share a common motivation. "It's a team job and the majority of our operators share the same passion as the people they're working with for being outdoors and doing sports activities," she says. "It's a fun job and that's why some of us are still here."

operators breaks, and keep an eye on the overall operation. The entire lift operation is managed by a supervisor.

While operating a lift isn't especially difficult, meticulous training in safety and customer service is required. You'll learn about routine operations as well as how to react to emergencies, but, luckily, you don't have to be a technician—the maintenance staff takes care of ski lift repairs.

Operators are taught to handle every conceivable emergency, such as fires, lift malfunctions, or brake problems. They're taught to evacuate passengers in case of a heavy storm, especially if lightning appears, and if they spot an injured skier, they're trained to call the ski patrol and keep the injured person comfortable. Even after they complete training and start working, operators undergo regular safety reviews. They're also taught how to treat guests; some ski lift operators are so cheerful and friendly that you'd think they were working at Disney World.

Lift operators usually enjoy free skiing during breaks, although that privilege may be based on job performance. Most lift operators work only during ski season and must look elsewhere for jobs during the spring and summer. If they want to remain in a resort area, many will work at golf courses in the warmer periods. Those who want a full-time job can apply for supervisory positions, which require a few years as a lift operator and at least some college background.

The work is a lot of fun, which is why plenty of ski lift operators have more trouble tearing themselves away from the job than finding one in the first place.

Pitfalls

The work is seasonal and most suitable for young singles. You'll be exposed to a lot of cold weather and hard work, and you may have trouble finding affordable housing in an upscale resort area.

Perks

If you're interested in being a ski operator, odds are you love to ski—so what could be better? You'll have the opportunity to be outdoors and ski for free. Most operators enjoy being part of a team and relish the sense of freedom and the social scene.

Get a Jump on the Job

Start skiing as early as you can. When you ride the lifts, pay attention to the operators. Note their personalities and how they treat you and other passengers. Get yourself fit enough to prepare for the job's physical demands.

SKYDIVING INSTRUCTOR

OVERVIEW

When first-time jumpers arrive at a sky-diving center, a lot of them have second thoughts. Maybe, they think, this wasn't as great an idea as it seemed a few days ago. "Maybe I'll get up in the plane and get terrified when I look down," they worry. "Maybe the parachute won't open." An instructor may not be able to put a student's mind totally at rest, but it's amazing what skilled training can do for a newcomer's attitude and nerves.

Thorough instruction is the key to safe and effective skydiving, which makes the skydiving instructor's job plenty important. As many as six hours at a skydiving school are spent trying to make sure that nobody becomes one of the 35 to 40 skydivers killed in an average year. Because of the risk, most schools require that jumpers be at least 18, and they must sign a waiver of liability so the center isn't held responsible for death or injury. Then the students are ready for class.

An instructor prepares new students for their first jump later that day, teaching them about their main and reserve parachutes and how wind affects a jump. They teach students how to react to equipment malfunctions and other emergencies, and how to land safely, and then they let students practice on a simulator. After students pass written, oral, or practical tests to show they've understood their class work, they're ready for a plane ride. They'll be flown over the drop zone, which is an open field often near a small airport.

A school may offer a *tandem freefall*, *solo accelerated freefall*, or *instant open-*

ing. On a tandem jump, the student and instructor are attached to one parachute system, and jump at between 10,000 and 13,000 feet, freefalling together for 30 to 50 seconds and then descending under a single large parachute with dual controls. A tandem jump is akin to an amusement park ride and little training is needed. On the solo accelerated freefall, a student leaves the aircraft at between 10,000 and 13,000 feet and freefalls with two instructors for 30 to 50 seconds. They keep a grip on the student's harness until the student opens the parachute, at about 4,000 feet. On the

Chris Hall, skydiving instructor

When Chris Hall sees a first-time jumper land safely, he's filled with pride and satisfaction. "It's like being a parent," he says. "I've got over 4,000 jumps and to see somebody make that first jump, you relive your first experience a little bit through their eyes. You see their excitement and smile and you're reminded of why you're in this business."

Hall, an instructor and owner of Skydive Kansas City, Inc., sometimes needs to be reminded why he's in skydiving. If he were interested in maximum income and minimum risk, he definitely would've headed for another line of work.

When Hall decided to start his skydiving center at Butler Memorial Airport in Missouri, he faced even more obstacles than other small business owners. Both his sport and business are considered so risky that banks wouldn't finance him and insurance companies wouldn't insure him. Hall raised money from friends and his father, John, and opened his center in 1998. He's known in the trade as a drop zone operator.

"You've got to love what you do and be ready for some ups and downs," Hall says. "One mistake can end a decade of hard work. There's no room for error in this business. If you're selling ice cream and you forget some chocolate chips, you'll tick a few people off. If you forget to pack a guy's chute properly and he winds up dead, you'll likely be in trouble for the rest of your life. Like my girlfriend says, 'It's like having a 2-year-old for the rest of your life.' You wake up with it in the morning and you put it to bed at night."

Hall has been around skydiving since he was two years old. That's when his father took up the sport after serving in Vietnam. John Hall would jump all day, and he passed his enthusiasm for the sport on to his son. When Chris turned 18, he made his first jump, and he's been jumping ever since. Because the sport is expensive, Hall became an instructor in Chicago so he could jump for free. He also studied his boss's operation and used it as his model when he opened his own business.

Hall employs 8 to 10 other instructors, but he still teaches and stays involved in every part of his business. He's certified as an instructor, pilot, parachute rigger, and mechanic. "I do whatever it takes to keep this operation moving," he explains. "It doesn't do any good if the pilot doesn't show and the student can't play. The student will go somewhere else or spend the money on something else."

The key, he says, is to know a little about everything. That takes a lot of time and requires getting a lot of ratings, but it's all about your commitment to the sport. "It's hard to maintain a healthy family life," he admits. "You're gone weekends, you work seven days a week. There are a lot of single guys running drop areas. To be in this business, you've got to really love skydiving."

Hall's overhead is steep. He periodically must replace 10 to 15 parachute systems, which cost $6,000 apiece. He also leases a Cessna 182, a popular skydiving plane. "It's an expensive business to operate," Hall says. "A guy once told me, 'If you want to make a million dollars in aviation, you'd better start with two million.' "

The stereotype of the first-time skydiver is somebody who's petrified with fear and won't jump out of the plane. How many such people does Hall come across? "Surprisingly, not many," he says. "Maybe two or three out of 100. Everybody shows up scared out of their minds. They didn't sleep, they're nervous, they're wondering what the heck they signed up for. But then they look around and see doctors, lawyers, and such a wide variety of people who enjoy the sport. When they come out of class, they see people coming back from their jumps and enjoying it. And then you see one of our first-timers do a solo jump and they're doing cartwheels on the field."

instant opening, students are helped out of the plane at 3,500 feet, and their parachute initially is attached to the plane by a 12-foot static line. Then the jumper is separated from the line and the parachute opens.

An instructor will usually take three jumpers in a plane. Skydivers are equipped with two-way radios, which allow an instructor on the ground to talk them down. As the first jumper is about to land, the second jumps, and the third jumper follows the same procedure. When all three are finished, the plane picks up another three jumpers.

After each jump, the instructor makes sure that each skydiver enters the date and instructor's name in a logbook. The jumpers receive certificates for making their first jump. They don't need more classroom training if they jump again within 60 days. Skydivers who jump after a long layoff are required to take a refresher course.

Because skydiving is a high-risk sport, instructors must be thoroughly trained and certified by the United States Parachute Association. Certification is obtained through course work, testing, and a required number of jumps. A "tandem master," an instructor certified to make tandem skydives, must have at least 500 dives, attend a tandem certification course, and must have spent at least three years in the sport.

Pitfalls

Skydiving instructors usually work weekends, which can put a strain on their family lives. There is also a certain amount of stress, since you're always one mistake away from seeing someone injured or killed.

Perks

Here's yet another job that allows you to make a living by pursuing your hobby. Instructors usually get to jump for free. There's a lot of satisfaction in helping people to overcome their fears and enjoy an exhilarating experience.

Get a Jump on the Job

The best way to get a jump on this job is to jump. You can jump anywhere in the United States once you turn 18. To learn more about the sport, you can read *Parachutist*, the magazine of the U.S. Parachute Association, or other skydiving magazines.

STADIUM VENDOR

OVERVIEW

Have you ever dreamed about getting paid to go to a ballgame or a rock concert? That's what vendors do, though they're bound to miss some plays or songs here and there while they're hiking up and down the stands, hawking food and drinks.

Stadium vendors work for a concessionaire—a company that holds a contract to sell food, drinks, souvenirs, programs, and yearbooks at a stadium or arena. If you've ever been to a ballgame and noticed hordes of hungry fans waiting in line to buy hot dogs, peanuts, and beer, you know what a great business concessions are.

But because these events usually last just a few hours, it wouldn't make sense for concessionaires to hire full-time vendors—so their sales force works part time, for extra income. Because most sports and entertainment events are held during evenings or weekends, most vendors can work at these events without disrupting their full-time job. You'll find vendors who keep their job for just a few months, and others who stay for decades. Time on the job is important, because the vendors who get to sell the best products in the best locations are the ones with the most seniority.

Vendors who've been at their job for many years can count on working any event they want. They usually get to sell the most profitable items and work in the most expensive seating areas. But some vendors show up for work not certain of

AT A GLANCE

Salary Range
$2,000 to $50,000

Education/Experience
You don't need a college degree, though many students help pay their tuition by working as a vendor during the summer. It helps to have experience in any kind of sales, especially to the public.

Personal Attributes
You need to have a loud voice and be willing to whoop and holler and call attention to yourself and your product. You should be friendly so customers will want to buy your items. You should be patient with fans who are slow deciding what they want or to getting out their money. You need to be observant so you can see a customer trying to catch your attention. You should feel comfortable dealing with people from many different walks of life.

Requirements
You'll need to demonstrate you can comfortably lift the load you'll be asked to carry. To sell beer, wine, or liquor, you'll have to obtain a special license and be of legal drinking age in your state.

Outlook
As long as fans pack stadiums and arenas for sports and entertainment, there will be jobs for vendors. This is one job that won't be replaced by machines or the Internet. For many fans, buying from a vendor is part of the fun of watching a ballgame.

being hired. The concessionaire usually can guess how big a staff will be needed for an event based on the weather, advance sales, and ticket lines, but sometimes vendors don't find out they're not needed until after they report for roll call.

Bob Reital, beer vendor

Selling beer in a ballpark may put pounds on his customers, but it sure takes them off Bob Reital. In fact, he looks like a different person when he's at the height of the sports season. When Reital gets his annual physical exam in early spring, his doctor always warns him that he's overweight. But once major league baseball starts, Reital loses as much weight as a dedicated Weight Watcher. Reital sells beer at Kansas City Royals games at Kauffman Stadium during the spring and summer and at Chiefs games at Arrowhead Stadium during fall and early winter. "I lose 20 pounds during the season," Reital says. "I see my doctor just before the Royals' season starts. He told me a few years ago that I looked pregnant. He doesn't see me in the latter part of the summer when I'm weighing 170 instead of 190."

If you watch Reital, it's easy to see why the weight rolls off. Whether he's carrying trays of beer, hot dog warmers, or a pile of pretzels, he gets a strenuous workout—especially when he's trudging up and down steep steps on a steamy summer night. It's common to see stadium vendors dripping with sweat as they lug their items up and down the stadium. Reital once tried saving time on refills by carrying two cases of beer instead of one, but found that 48 bottles, the ice, and a tray were too heavy a load. "That'll kill you," he says.

The loads feel heaviest at the start of the season. "You don't have to be Arnold Schwarznegger," Reital says. "When I started out, I thought there was no way I could do this. But you will build up to where you can." Reital has learned to be adaptable because he's held so many different jobs. He's delivered phone books, transported railroad crews, sacked groceries, installed cable TV, and cut lumber—until the day he answered a newspaper ad for stadium vendors in 2003 and was hired by Centerplate, the concessionaire for both Royals' and Chiefs' games. He had to get a special license to sell beer, usually a hot seller. "Some days it is, some days it isn't," he says philosophically. "Some days you're the windshield. Sometimes you're the bug."

Although he's usually hustling, Reital generally sees most of a baseball game. "Whether they're winning or losing, I love the atmosphere," he says. But his income does depend on whether the home team is winning or losing. When the Royals hit hard times, crowds fell off, and so did beer sales. The Chiefs, however, usually draw crowds of almost 80,000, and Reital can sell 10 cases of beer during a game. "Every day is a good day at a Chiefs' game," he says. However, a beer vendor has to remember when to stop selling. To cut down on the number of intoxicated fans who may be driving home, the Royals stop selling beer after the eighth inning and the Chiefs stop after the third quarter. Reital leaves the stands quickly so he doesn't have to argue with fans who might demand a beer after the deadline. He's also expected to refuse to serve any customer who appears to be drunk.

Reital knows he's going to have a good night at a baseball game when customers empty his first case of beer while he's still walking from the commissary to his section in the upper deck. He's also sold bottled water, soda, and peanuts, but couldn't get the hang of tossing a peanut bag. If a customer is seated in the middle of a row, the peanut vendor usually throws the bag like a baseball and the customer is supposed to catch it. "I sold peanuts once and smacked a guy in the face," Reital says. "I says: 'I'm not doing this anymore.' It's tough, especially when you can't pitch!"

Once a vendor has been picked to work, it's off to the cash window to get change and put on a uniform, and then on to a com-missary (the area where food and drink is stocked). The vendor picks up the first batch of items and gives the commissary manager a ticket to account for the load, and then tries to get to the stands before the event starts.

Some vendors develop a distinctive selling style. By having a catch phrase, a rhyme or joke, or a sing-song way of hawking their product, vendors can become so popular that customers want to buy especially from them. Vendors, in that sense, are like any other salespeople. The most successful ones figure out how to separate themselves from the rest.

If there's a big crowd, vendors might sell their first batches of food or drinks quickly. On a slow night, it might seem like forever until they're sold out. Once the supply is empty, the vendor returns to the commissary for another load. At the end of the event, the vendor turns in the money to a cash office and receives a commission for each item sold; they get a check after their receipts are totaled. They also may be eligible for a year-end bonus. (Employees at concession stands, however, are paid by the hour.)

Most vendors try to increase their income by working more than one type of event. Even a major league baseball team, which plays 162 games, is home only half the time between April and September, so a vendor might work several venues and for more than one concessionaire. In a city such as New York, Boston, or Chicago, a vendor might be able to choose among jobs for major league baseball, pro and college football, pro basketball, pro hockey, auto racing, concerts, and circuses.

Pitfalls

You're not always guaranteed work, and it can be exhausting carrying heavy trays or containers up and down steps, especially on a hot night.

Perks

You can see a lot of great events for free while making extra income—all still working at your full-time job. You can have some really good days if you're selling a popular product at a big football game or auto race drawing crowds of 80,000 or more.

Get a Jump on the Job

The next time you attend a stadium or arena event, take a first-hand look at what it's like to be a vendor. Observe them as they walk up and down the aisles and make their sales pitches. If you're of high school age, apply to a concessionaire for a job.

THEME PARK CHARACTER

OVERVIEW

We all remember that first magical glimpse of Mickey Mouse, Goofy, or Minnie Mouse at the Magic Kingdom—or the walking Mr. Chocolate Bar at Hershey Park. As a child, how wonderful it was to look up to this magical creature, suddenly come to life, many times our size!

For some people, they've never gotten over their fascination with theme parks and the special characters who inhabit them—and if this sounds like you, theme park character might be the career for you.

It's not necessarily easy to land the position, however. Everyone must audition to become a character, a process that can last up to 10 hours; specific heights are often a deciding factor. Typically, actors should have lots of personality, be animated, have acting ability, and truly enjoy interacting with children. Auditioning characters may be asked to dance or mime. For Disney "face" characters, actors should look something like the characters and be the correct height (typically, males should be between 5'9" and 6'1" and females should be between 5'3" and 5'9").

Once you make the cut, you're typically sent to "character school" for a week or two to learn all you can about the character. Then it's time to don the costume and head out into the park. Typically, your job is to interact with park visitors (usually—but not always—the kids), mugging for photos, dancing, walking hand in hand, and signing autographs. In some theme parks, the

---

AT A GLANCE

Salary Range

$10 to $25 an hour, depending on park and type of character.

Education/Experience

There's no college major for "theme park character," but you've got to have some kind of talent or experience to land these jobs. Acting experience, dancing ability, and mime talents will help.

Personal Attributes

You must love kids, get along well with all kinds of people, be able to withstand high temperatures in stuffy costumes, and have a great sense of humor.

Requirements

Typically, characters must be at least 17 years old and at least a graduating high school senior; most characters must meet certain height requirements.

Outlook

Good. Continuing popularity of theme parks across the United States (and a growing contingent of characters) ensures a continuing need for theme park characters.

---

characters take on extra duties, appearing at special "character breakfasts" or popping up in parades or special events.

Pitfalls

Yes, it's true, it's *hot* in those costumes—and most characters work during the summer months, when things can get really stifling. (Characters in southern areas, such as in Florida, can really bake in July and August.)

Perks

If you love kids—and you're a kid at heart—what could be more fun than dressing up

John Doe*, former Disney character actor

Ever since his first peek at the Magic Kingdom as a lad, John Doe was fascinated by this magical world of fantasy brought to life. "There was the giant lot where you parked your car in Goofy 12 or Pluto 22, the tram and the monorail, and then you finally arrived," he recalls. "It was an awesome experience to walk through the front gates, under the train and onto Main Street; smelling the popcorn, listening to the barber shop quartet, rushing to the rides."

Wherever he went in the park, he always noticed the characters—Mickey, Minnie, Goofy— living, breathing, moving. "They were the larger-than-life inhabitants of this magical world that was, in itself, larger-than-life," he recalls. "I was mesmerized by the characters. From the way they interacted with the crowds to the personal escort always at their side, they were genuine celebrities."

After graduation from college, armed with an advertising degree but no job on Madison Avenue, Doe happened upon a Disney ad for character performers in the "help wanted" section. The auditions were held at a soundstage far away from the theme park, attracting a huge number of people anxious to don the costume of one of their Disney heroes. After dancing and miming ("Show me 'trying on a pair of shoes but putting them on the wrong feet and walking around'!") he got the job, and was placed at the Magic Kingdom. It was off to the Magic Kingdom orientation program, where for two weeks he learned about the characters he'd be playing (a decision determined by height). At the end of the two weeks, each person must pass an exam based on how much you know of the characters and your ability to sign their names. (Character signatures must be identical.)

"The best part was definitely seeing the smiles on the guests' faces," he says. "People of all ages react in an amazing way for the characters. They almost disappear into a fantasy world where they believe they are actually meeting Goofy or Donald Duck—it's incredible. So being able to bring this character to life to seeing the positive effect it had on people . . . that was definitely the best part of the job."

That doesn't mean it was all cotton candy and chocolate cake. "The worst part of the job was obnoxious teenagers who would try to push you around or look underneath the character head," he observes.

During his stint in the Magic Kingdom, he portrayed five different characters. To make extra money, he'd work extra shifts at one of the other parks or at a hotel character breakfast. In the end, he worked about four months in the Magic Kingdom. "Some people remain in their jobs for 10 years and this is their career," he says. "Other people do it as a job for a few months, either on a college program or people who have just always wanted to do it and are finally getting the opportunity."

There was a lot to learn as a character. "There's a definite pecking order among character performers at Disney," Doe says. "At the top of the food chain are the face characters [unmasked performers who portray characters such as Cinderella and Prince Charming]. "They're the stars of the show and rarely associate with anyone outside their circle. Further down the ladder, you've got your 'Main 5,' which includes the five classic Disney characters, Mickey, Minnie, Goofy, Donald, and Pluto. Everybody else is below that."

(continues)

(continued)

If you'd like to become a Disney character actor, you need to be full of enthusiasm and spirit. "Disney takes everything seriously, as they should," Doe explains. "When they hire someone to play a character, they realize the huge responsibility this person is going to be taking on. For example, even when you're having a bad day or you're exhausted or you just don't feel like performing, you have to do it. You have to do it because that's what the guests are paying for and that's what the guests have come to expect. So you put all the baggage away and go out there and perform and give the guests something they're going to remember; whether it's a fun photo or interacting with children or whatever. Disney wants people who can do that—who will go above and beyond to have fun in the job and to make memorable experiences for the guests."

If you're good at dancing and choreography, you'll probably be picked out to be a character who performs in parades and shows, he notes. If you're good at miming or acting things out, you'll also stand a good chance of being selected to be a character.

"It's been several years since my exposure to backstage Disney," Doe says, "and going to the park every single day did not diminish my love for the Magic Kingdom. I still turn into that young boy whenever I walk through the front gates down Main Street and I still rush to stand in line at Space Mountain. In fact, having worked at Disney and going behind the scenes only fed my craving to be part of the magic."

It remains a deeply satisfying time in his life. "It was wonderful," he says. "I can't say enough good things about my time there or about Disney in general. Say what you will about this huge corporation, but they are still incredibly dedicated to Walt's vision of creating a magical place for families. And for me to be a part of that place was a wonderful experience."

---

*Not his real name.

---

completely and becoming somebody else? Interacting with the crowds, free parking, and first dibs on riding the new rides are other perks that theme park characters enjoy.

Get a Jump on the Job

If you're intrigued by this job, you can practice by participating in your school plays and by trying out for a job as a school mascot. Visit lots of theme parks and watch how the chararcters inteact with guests, how they move and communicate. Try out for a summer job as a character at a theme park near your home.

THEME PARK MANAGER

OVERVIEW

Few of us grow up without visiting a theme park, whether a small one off a lonely highway exit or a huge, multi-theme park smack in a major tourist area. Chances are you've been one of those visitors who go on a favorite ride time after time and can't be dragged away until closing time.

So if you're going to stay at a theme park all day anyway, you might consider getting paid. As a general manager of a smaller theme park, you may oversee the whole enchilada; in a bigger park, the general manager will have assistants in charge of key departments. But whether your responsibilities are large or small, probably one of the most enjoyable things you'll do is picking the rides. When you're deciding what rides your park will include, you'll first need to consider rides that are compatible with the park's theme and customers. Some parks may emphasize roller coasters—and the bigger and faster and scarier they are, the better. But if you're going to include roller coasters, they still need to fit a park's theme. For example, when Disney World included a high-thrill roller coaster, it cast it as a space adventure in Tomorrowland and called it Space Mountain. But you wouldn't want a space ride in a Wild West park.

On the other hand, many parks cater to too many small fry and grandparents to have high-thrill roller coasters.

So if you manage a park, how do you pick a new ride? You might start by surveying your customers—old ones, new ones, and some who've never been to your park. Ask them what kinds of rides make them want to beat down your door. Then you and your staff can consider the results and discuss which kind of ride to pursue. You might remember a ride that was a big

Jason Bernard, director of attractions

As an executive at Silver Dollar City in the tourist hot spot of Branson, Missouri, Jason Bernard finds his college degree worthless and priceless at the same time. It's worthless because to advance up the ladder, his on-the-job training meant everything, but his degree is valuable because Bernard has found that his old career and current one have a lot in common. He graduated from Old Dominion University in Virginia with degrees in secondary education and social studies, and taught for two years at York High School in Virginia while he also worked at Busch Gardens in Williamsburg.

"A lot of what I was doing in high school involved the same principles as working in Busch Gardens," Bernard said. "If you're teaching somebody the capital of Zaire or teaching them to tighten a harness, you're still educating them. I just found over the years that a lot of what I was applying as a high school teacher was what I was applying as a supervisor in the parks world."

He started as a "cast member" at Busch Gardens when he was 20. "We always refer to our parks as 'putting on a show,' and we were called cast members," Bernard recalled. "I worked on the Roman Rapids. I started one spring break and the rest is history. I'm where I am because of my experience, not my degree. This is one business where experience really helps you."

Once he chose a career in theme parks, Bernard moved to Six Flags Kentucky Kingdom in Louisville, and then Busch Gardens in Tampa. From there, it was on to Silver Dollar City, an 1880s theme park that operates March through December. The park opened in 1955 as a replica of a 19th-century Ozark Mountains village and sits on top of Marvel Cave, a tourist attraction since 1894. Bernard wanted to find a roller coaster that could provide thrills but also fit the park's theme and not scare away the five- and six-year-olds who flock to Silver Dollar City. "We're more family-oriented, we're not here to scare you," he said. "We weren't looking for a roller coaster that was 400 feet high and could get from zero to 100 miles per hour in three seconds. We want people who are 42 inches tall to ride it and not fear it."

Bernard helped come up with the PowderKeg. It cost $10 million to manufacture and uses compressed air to launch riders from zero to 53 miles per hour in 2.8 seconds. The ride is named for the powder produced by nitrogen-rich bat guano mined from Marvel Cave in the 1880s. PowderKeg starts in a powder mill amid barrels of explosives that rock and tip. The barrels then explode and the car blasts out of the building with special effects of fire and smoke. The car climbs to a 110-foot drop, then goes into banked turns and through a wave of hills, in which riders feel weightlessness. A trip lasts nearly three minutes and spirals around six acres on 3,500 feet of track. With 16 passengers per train, PowderKeg can carry more than 1,000 people per hour.

"These rides are not built as they were 30 years ago," Bernard said. "We have a very similar system to NASA's . . . with sensors on the tracks that tell us if it's a 'go' or 'no go.'" If something's off in terms of millimeters or milliseconds, the ride operators have to react.

"Any given day is exciting and unique," he says. "You don't know what you'll be facing." Perhaps a ride will be closed all day, or lots of employees call in sick. Maybe it's raining when the forecast was for 80 percent sunshine. "I've always prided myself on my ability to think on my feet," he says. "You work long hours, especially in the summer. But when you sit at the exit at the end of the night and see all those smiling faces, it's also a lot of fun."

hit at another park where you've worked, or you might get ideas for new rides by visiting other parks with a customer base similar to yours. Or you might visit the huge trade show held each year by the International Association of Amusement Parks and Attractions and see if any exhibitors have the kind of ride you need. Finally, you could hire a manufacturer to make you your very own perfect ride—so that not only will you have a popular ride, but an original one, too.

In choosing a ride, you'll consider the "thrill factor," which is the ride's excitement, fun, and ability to make a customer want to ride it again. You'll consider how many passengers you want your ride to handle in an hour. The world's most exciting ride won't help your park much if few customers get a chance to hop aboard. And you'll want to consider the ride's operation, maintenance, and safety. Theme park managers emphasize safety because they're responsible for customers' well-being. And an accident on a ride might injure people, damage a park's reputation, and invite lawsuits.

A theme park may seem like a simple place to customers, but not to those who manage them. In addition to the rides, managers supervise exhibits and games, ticket booths, entrances and exits, parking lots, concession stands, baby stroller rentals, guest relations, and security. They also oversee the finance-related departments and of course, supervise employees, from seasonal help to full-time staffers.

Managing a theme park has little in common with enjoying the rides, except that both customers and managers wouldn't care to spend their day anywhere else.

Pitfalls

You'll work long hours and won't have many days off during busy season, and you won't make a lot of money at first, when you start at the bottom of the ladder. You should expect headaches like mechanical problems and bad weather.

Perks

The atmosphere is terrific because you're working with people who are having a good time. There's tremendous satisfaction in seeing a park's attractions, departments, and employees working together. And the job's variety will keep you hopping.

Get a Jump on the Job

Theme parks couldn't exist without the teenagers who work during weekends and all summer. These jobs don't pay much better than minimum wage but will give you a feel for a park's operation and atmosphere. Many managers have started at this level.

WINE CONSULTANT

OVERVIEW

Everywhere you look, interest in wine is growing. Whether people dine at home or in restaurants, many enjoy a glass of wine with their meals. Many wine shops and art galleries offer free wine samples on special nights, and both casual and serious wine buyers order wine from stores, catalogs, wine clubs, or on the Internet. Towns and cities hold wine festivals to boost tourism.

You might think that with so many people drinking wine, selling wine would be easy, right? Actually, a lot of winemakers have trouble selling their product because there's so much competition around the world. A winery may know how to make a great wine, but may not be so savvy about getting it on a store's shelf or onto a restaurant's wine list. That's why wineries (especially smaller ones) hire wine consultants. If you think you'd enjoy helping a winemaker improve business, wine consulting could be just the job for you.

A winery usually needs to find a distributor, the middleman between the producer and retailer. The distributor buys the wine from the winemaker and sells it to the retailer, who sells it to the customer. A consultant can help a winery find a distributor, and if the winery is overseas, also an importer. Those who connect a winery with an importer, distributor, or retail store are known as wine brokers. The wine broker could be a large company or merely an independent consultant.

AT A GLANCE

Salary Range
$40,000 to $60,000

Education/Experience
A college degree isn't a must, but you'll need to know sales and marketing. You'll also need an education in wine, either in college or by working in a business where wine is produced or sold.

Personal Attributes
You must get along well with people and show winemakers that you know your business. You must be a good listener and understand a client's needs. If you're in business for yourself, you must be able to deal with the risks that face any entrepreneur. Because wine is a global business, you must be comfortable dealing with clients from different cultures.

Requirements
You'll need a vast amount of knowledge about wine and an enthusiasm for this business.

Outlook
This is a growing industry. U.S. wine sales have been increasing since 1990, so the number of winemakers who need consultants should also keep increasing.

So how can selling wine get so complicated? Don't all wines just come from grapes? How different can they be?

The fact is, two different wines can be fundamentally different; depending on the grapes, soil, climate, rainfall, storage, and aging, wines can vary in taste, quality, and price. There are red, white, and blush wines. There are table, dessert, and sparkling wines. Fancy restaurants with extensive wine lists may offer bottles that

Laura Bishop, wine consultant

Laura Bishop was studying hotel and restaurant management at Cornell University in Ithaca, New York, when she began her career in wine—she asked the owner of a nearby winery if she could work there as an intern.

"The owner said, 'That would be fantastic,'" recalled Bishop, now an independent wine consultant who lives in Big Sur, south of California wine country. "I was a bottler on the bottling line, worked in the field, worked in the tasting room, was a sales rep, and even drove the delivery van. I did a little bit of everything."

Once she graduated from Cornell, Bishop could've explored many avenues in the hotel and restaurant businesses. Instead, she became a wine steward for a hotel in Atlanta and has worked in the wine industry ever since. "This was clearly the most fun part of the [hotel and restaurant] industry," she said. "It's the nature of wine that intrigues me. Wine is alive. A bottle of rosé would be different than any other rosé in the world, even if it's from the same vintner. It's different than it would be a year earlier or six months later. Wine had a life of its own and I realized I would never know all I need to know about it. That hooked me."

Bishop then became a sales manager for a wine brokerage company in Atlanta. She eventually moved to Napa, in California wine country, and her employers there included a small winery and a huge distributor. She often brushed shoulders with people who were lured to California by the technology gold rush, yet seemed fascinated by Bishop's specialty. "I would frequently be surrounded by Apple computer employees at parties and they'd be making scads more money than me," she recalled. "But they'd say, 'You're in the wine industry, that's so much fun.' Those of us in the wine industry are in it because we love it."

Bishop went back to school to earn a master of business administration degree from the Monterey Institute of International Studies. By 1998, she was ready to go out on her own. She decided she could find her niche as a consultant to overseas wineries trying to break into the highly-profitable yet highly-competitive U.S. market. She founded a consulting firm, Peregrine Strategies.

"It's the kind of thing I foresaw as a need, but that nobody else was addressing," she said. "I was like Florence Nightingale, coming to the rescue of small wineries overseas. Wine is at once farming and art. At the glamour end, it's a lifestyle statement—people put wine in their cellars and hold it as if it was an investment, like artwork. A lot of my clients are actual growers, they're farmers. I can't think of another industry where you have that combination of people, and I have worked with both. You can have as little or as much fun as you want. My niche is people having fun. I became this obscure winery crusader because people going small were getting lost in the mix."

Bishop consults wineries in Australia, New Zealand, Greece, and Argentina. A winery may excel at marketing its wines at home but find it needs a different sales strategy for U.S. customers. "I'm a private service that helps small businesses do market entry," she said. "A winery comes to me and pays me to be the matchmaker, so I help the winery find a good importer. It became clear very quickly that people needed a leg up to know how things work over here. They need more guidance—like how our pricing works. Coming from Argentina, you might not have an idea of a label that is

(continues)

(continued)

attractive to Americans. You might think that a green and orange label is great, but you need it to be more attractive and upscale. They're unfamiliar with American cultural standards and how they do business here."Consulting gives Bishop a golden opportunity to mix her business education with love of wines. "People say, 'You didn't really need your MBA, did you?' "But I prefer to have it," she said. "You have to have a good palate but you also have to understand marketing. There's a lot of wine out there of great quality but different from what Americans want to buy. I'm able to spot wine that's technically good and find how we can make it appealing in this market. It won't do me or the winery any good if they have wines that are not going to fly. I worked with a New Zealand firm that was unable to find a U.S. importer. I helped them put a package together. They were bought out by Gallo and they're on their sailboats now. I did so well, they're no longer working."

Bishop in a typical year makes about three overseas and four or five domestic trips. "I enjoy the travel and cross-cultural aspect and I have a lot to offer," she said. "There are always jobs for people who know how to connect with other people. If wines are what you love, do that. I love the idea of being a freelancer. For me, it's a marvelous lifestyle and a great way to make a living."

---

cost more than $100. That's why a wine consultant must know a cheap wine from an expensive wine and which wines will please which kinds of customers. But a cheap wine doesn't have to be unpopular. In fact, the cheapest wines, known as "extreme-value" wines, are very popular throughout the United States, which is the world's largest wine market.

Some consultants become wine experts by working for restaurants, bars, wine shops, or wineries. Others study business to learn about sales and marketing, as well as about wine. Several colleges offer degrees in enology, the study of wine. The University of California–Davis is considered the nation's top wine school. But you can learn about wine in many countries, and some winemakers have become international consultants for other wineries. These consultants are called "flying winemakers."

A huge winery, like the E. & J. Gallo Winery in California, doesn't have a hard time getting its wine distributed. In fact, Gallo sells so much wine at popular prices

that any distributor will jump at the chance to handle Gallo wines. Small wineries, however, may struggle to get noticed, and that's when they'll turn to a consultant for help. A consultant may advise a winery to adjust its prices to become more appealing, or recommend a different label for the bottles. The consultant may line up a distributor who will put the wine in retail stores and restaurants, or suggest advertising or public relations strategies to make a winery better known.

A good consultant knows that it's one thing to grow grapes, but quite another thing to grow a wine business. The better a consultant is at growing others' wine businesses, the more money they'll earn.

Pitfalls

An independent consultant faces the same insecurities and stress as any self-employed person. There's no regular paycheck or company benefits. And if wineries are paying for your know-how, they won't keep you if you don't help their business.

Perks

If you enjoy travel, you'll love visiting clients, especially if they're overseas. If you're a wine enthusiast, this is the chance to turn your hobby into a career.

Get a Jump on the Job

Take business courses, especially in sales and marketing. You can work as a clerk in a wine shop, once you reach the legal age in your state. Until then, you can search the Internet or visit your local library for information about wineries, vineyards, and how wines are produced. When you're in college, you can major in enology or check out your chances of working as a summer intern at a winery.

APPENDIX A. ASSOCIATIONS, ORGANIZATIONS, AND WEB SITES

GENERAL

International Association for the Leisure and Entertainment Industry
10 Briarcrest Square
Hershey, PA 17033
(888) 464-6498
http://www.ialei.org/you

The IALEI is a nonprofit association that focuses on helping members be more successful in their businesses. IALEI helps members maximize results in an individual attraction and shows members how to make them work together to give a better result. IALEI members include family entertainment centers, laser tag centers, batting cages, arcades, golf courses, bowling greens, ice skating centers, paintball fields, action sport parks, skateboard parks, children's museums, miniature golf courses, children's entertainment centers, sports parks, water parks, campgrounds, amusement parks, and roller skating centers.

AERIALIST

American Youth Circus Organization
PO Box 96
Temple, NH 03084
(603) 654-5523
info@americanyouthcircus.org
http://www.americanyouthcircus.org

AYCO promotes youth participation in circus arts. Its showcase event is the biennial international AYCO Festival. The festival includes workshops, discussion groups, performances by youth troupes from around North America, and special performances by circus stars of the future. AYCO also fosters communication among circus arts educators and organizations; provides circus arts coaches with training procedures and guidelines for safety standards; provides support for artistic performers wishing to pursue or expand their circus careers; promotes youth circus activities through public relations efforts and a biannual newsletter; and provides circus-related educational materials to schools and educators.

Circus Fans Association of America
2704 Marshall Avenue
Lorain, OH 44052-04315
http://www.circusfans.org

The CFA was established in 1926 to enjoy and preserve the circus as an institution. This original goal is still the cornerstone of the organization. Members also monitor federal, state, and local legislation, and they sometimes find themselves involved case by case—testifying at hearings, passing out educational pamphlets, and keeping the public informed. The organization also produces a magazine six times a year.

The Circus Shop
http://www.circusshop.net/
The Web site offers a selection of circus equipment, books, and videos, available primarily by mail order.

The Circus Space
Coronet Street
London, N1 6HD

United Kingdom
+44 (0)20 7613 4141
http://www.thecircusspace.co.uk/

This registered charity specializes in the circus arts and is one of the top three circus schools in Europe. It is a member of the European Federation of Circus Schools and the United Kingdom's Circus Arts Forum. Circus Space offers a diverse artistic program that includes the only degree-level education in the circus arts in the United Kingdom, professional development opportunities for aspiring and established performers, participatory and leisure activities for young people and adults, and a varied performance program, including the annual Circus Space Festival. The group also provides affordable workspace for related arts companies and opportunities for private and public sector organizations to use circus skills as a staff development tool.

Flying Trapeze Resource Page
http://www.damnhot.com/trapeze/

A complete resource for the flying trapeze enthusiast, with information on flying trapeze clubs, schools, resorts, acrobatics, circus, gymnastics, and juggling.

AUCTIONEER

American Society of Auctioneers
4470 Chamblee Dunworthy Road
Suite 150, Classroom A
Atlanta, GA 30338
(770) 220-0095
http://www.actitrain.com

The American Society of Auctioneers serves licensed auction practitioners. Services to members include eligibility to enroll, for a fee, in an 80-hour course in pre-licensing education for those who want to work in the auction industry. Those who successfully complete the course receive a certificate of completion.

The association also offers an eight-hour continuing education course for auctioneers who practice in Georgia. Classes are held at the American Career Training Institute in Atlanta. The institute also offers other courses helpful to auctioneers, such as personal property appraisal and real estate appraisal. In addition to certificates for course work, certain professional certifications and designations are available to all active members of the auctioneers' society.

Auctioneer's Society of Certified Appraisers
554 W. State Road 42
Mooresville, IN 46158
(317) 996-2402
http://www.midwayauctionschool.com/
maina.htm

The goal of the society is, through education and collaboration of members, to enhance the knowledge and proficiency of professional auctioneers in the practice of personal property appraising, and to increase service to the public through a correct and competent personal property appraisal.

Christie's
20 Rockefeller Plaza
New York, NY 10020
(212) 636-2000
http://www.christies.com

Exemplary client service and extensive experience are the two most important assets that have fueled Christie's success as an auction house. This commitment to excellence began in the auction house's early years when James Christie conducted his first sale on December 5, 1766. Since its founding, Christie's auctions have been major attractions, and today Christie's salerooms continue to be a popular showcase for the unique and the beautiful.

National Auctioneers Association
8880 Ballentine
Overland Park, KS 66214
(913) 541-8084
http://www.auctioneers.org

The National Auctioneers Association promotes the auction method of marketing and enhances the professionalism of its practitioners. NAA member auctioneers are at the top of their field in the auction business. Ethical, accredited, and technology-savvy, NAA members are professionals well versed in the psychology of selling. Their education, experience, and networking capabilities stimulate competition among bidders, securing you the highest price per sale.

National Auto Auction Association
5320-D Spectrum Drive
Frederick, MD 21703
(301) 696-0400
http://www.naaa.com

The NAAA has 360 recurring member auctions in 19 countries, and offers information and Web site details about the auto auction business.

Sotheby's
1334 York Avenue
New York, NY 10021
(541) 312-5682
http://search.sothebys.com/

The largest and one of the oldest fine art auctioneers in the world, with more than 100 Sotheby's offices around the world; and, in 1998, auction sales that produced a turnover of just under $2 billion.

CASINO DEALER

American Gaming Association
555 13th Street NW, Suite 1010 East
Washington, DC 20004
(202) 637-6500

info@americangaming.org
http://www.americangaming.org

The AGA represents the commercial casino entertainment industry by addressing federal legislative and regulatory issues, such as federal taxation and travel and tourism matters. In addition, the AGA has an aggressive public education program designed to bring the industry's message to target audiences both in the nation's capital and across the country. The AGA provides leadership in addressing newly emerging national issues and in developing industrywide programs on critical issues such as disordered and underage gambling. The association also serves as the industry's first national information clearinghouse, providing the media, elected officials, other decision makers and the public with timely, accurate gaming industry data.

Casino Careers Online
http://www.casino-dealers.com/

Online resource for individuals looking for jobs in the casino industry, where potential employees can post a resume for free in a secure database, applying online directly to casinos.

Casino Dealer College
The Casino College
870 Market Street, Suite #838
San Francisco, CA
(916) 366-3589
info@ideal21.com
http://www.casinodealercollege.com

The Casino Dealer College is California's largest and northern California's oldest casino school, which teaches prospective dealers everything they need to know to become a professional dealer in as little as two weeks. Course options include poker dealing, seven card stud, blackjack, pai gow, and pai gow tiles. Students who complete a casino training program are fully certified professional casino dealers.

Casinoworker.com

http://www.casinoworker.com/

The site lists available jobs and the ability to post a resume for one month for free. The Web site's goal is to provide a virtual tour of Las Vegas.

National Indian Gaming Association

http://www.indiangaming.org/

The National Indian Gaming Association (NIGA), established in 1985, is a nonprofit organization of 184 Indian nations and associate members representing organizations, tribes, and businesses engaged in tribal gaming enterprises. NIGA is dedicated to advancing the lives of Indian people economically, socially, and politically. The group operates as a clearinghouse and educational, legislative, and public policy resource for tribes, policymakers, and the public on Indian gaming issues and tribal community development.

Off Shore Gaming Association

(877) 742-6742

http://www.osga.com

The Off Shore Gaming Association (OSGA) is an independent watchdog agency that monitors the off shore sports gaming industry in an effort to provide the public with a way to find reputable gaming companies.

CLUB MED HOST

Club Med Jobs

Club Med—North America
75 Valencia Avenue, 12th Floor
Coral Gables, FL 33134
resumes@clubmed.com
http://www.clubmedjobs.com

Web site listing corporate and village jobs, information about living conditions, audition tips, events, and applications, along with information about the Club Med history.

CONVENTION PLANNER

Association of Destination Management Executives

3333 Quebec Street, Suite 4050
Denver, CO 80207
(937) 586-3727
http://www.adme.org

The Association of Destination Management Executives (ADME) is the only global nonprofit association dedicated to increasing the professionalism and effectiveness of destination management through education, promotion of ethical practices, and availability of information to the meetings, convention, and incentive travel industries, as well as the general public.

Convention Industry Council

8201 Greensboro Drive, Suite 300
McLean, VA 22102
http://www.conventionindustry.org

The Convention Industry Council's 30 member organizations represent more than 100,000 individuals, as well as 15,000 firms and properties involved in the meetings, conventions, and exhibitions industries. Formed in 1949 to provide a forum for member organizations seeking to enhance the industry, the CIC facilitates the exchange of information and develops programs to promote professionalism with the industry and educates the public on its profound economic impact. In addition to the CMP Program, CIC is also responsible for the Hall of Leaders Program as well as the Accepted Practices Exchange (APEX).

APEX is working to unite the entire meeting, convention, and exhibition industry in the development and eventual implementation of voluntary standards, which will be called accepted practices.

International Special Events Society
401 North Michigan Avenue
Chicago, IL 60611
(312) 321-6853
http://www.ises.com

The International Special Events Society is comprised of more than 4,000 professionals in over a dozen countries representing special event producers (from festivals to trade shows), caterers, decorators, florists, destination management companies, rental companies, special effects experts, tent suppliers, audio-visual technicians, party and convention coordinators, balloon artists, educators, journalists, hotel sales managers, specialty entertainers, convention center managers, and many more.

Meeting Professionals International
4455 LBJ Freeway, Suite 1200
Dallas, TX 75244
(972) 702-3000
http://www.mpiweb.org

Established in 1972, Dallas-based Meeting Professionals International (MPI) is the largest association for the meetings profession with more than 20,000 members in 66 chapters and clubs. As the global authority and resource for the meetings and events industry, MPI empowers meeting professionals to increase their strategic value through education, clearly defined career pathways, and business growth opportunities.

The Professional Convention Management Association
2301 South Lake Shore Drive, Suite 1001

Chicago, IL 60616
(312) 423-7262
http://www.pcma.org

The Professional Convention Management Association (PCMA) is a nonprofit international association of professionals in the meetings industry whose mission is to deliver breakthrough education and promote the value of professional convention management.

CORPORATE CONCIERGE

International Concierge and Errand Association
4932 Castor Avenue
Philadelphia, PA 19124
(215) 743-5618
http://iceaweb.org

The International Concierge and Errand Association (ICEA) is a nonprofit trade association founded in 2001 designed to meet the professional needs of Concierge and Errand business owners worldwide. ICEA offers members business support, networking opportunities, continuing education, advocacy, and industry recognition. ICEA is the leading global professional association committed to supporting the owners and operators of concierge and errand service businesses, serving as the primary resource and active advocate for our members through essential resources, continuing education, networking opportunities, and other professional endeavors.

National Concierge Association
(612) 317-2932
info@nationalconciergeassociation.com
http://www.nationalconciergeassociation.com

The National Concierge Association (NCA) grants membership status to concierge professionals and vendors alike.

Southern Nevada Hotel Concierge Association
2961 Industrial Road, Suite 636
Las Vegas, NV 89109
(702) 990-2570
http://snhca.com/

The Southern Nevada Hotel Concierge Association is committed to providing the best customer service to hotel visitors staying in the Las Vegas / Southern Nevada area. The association aims to promote, educate, and maintain the high standards of the concierge, while building strong professional and personal relationships with fellow concierges, hotels, and businesses in the community. It offers exemplary service through job knowledge of services available within Las Vegas and Southern Nevada and by showing a genuine care and sensitivity to guests.

Washington Area Concierge Association
PO Box 167
1200 Pennsylvania Avenue, NW
Washington, DC 20044
http://www.wacaonline.com/

The Washington Area Concierge Association fosters opportunities to promote educational and professional growth for concierges both within and beyond the organization. WACA upholds a standard of integrity and ethics for concierges both within and beyond the organization, striving to achieve a greater respect for the concierge profession and encouraging friendships and solidarity among the concierges of all hotels and buildings in the Washington area. The association tries to develop a stronger working relationship with area businesses and cultural organizations to promote the Washington Area Concierge Association and tourism in general for the greater Washington area.

CRUISE SHIP ACTIVITY DIRECTOR

Cruise Lines International Association
80 Broad Street, Suite 1800
New York, NY 10004
(212) 921-0066
http://www.cruising.org/About.cfm

Cruise Lines International Association is a marketing and training organization composed of 19 of the major cruise lines serving North America. CLIA was formed in 1975 in response to a need for an association to promote the special benefits of cruising. CLIA exists to educate, train, promote, and explain the value, desirability, and affordability of the cruise vacation experience.

Cruise Line Jobs
http://www.cruiselinejob.com

Web site offering specific information about cruise line jobs.

Cruise Job Line
http://www.cruisejobline.com/

Cruise Job Line has been successfully serving both job seekers and the cruise industry since 1999, placing new personnel with cruise lines including Royal Caribbean, Carnival Cruise Lines, Norwegian Cruise Line, Holland America Line, Princess Cruises, Costa Cruise Lines, Celebrity Cruises, Crystal Cruises, American Hawaii Cruises, Cunard Line, Radisson Seven Seas Cruises, and Windstar Cruises.

Florida-Caribbean Cruise Association
11200 Pines Boulevard, Suite 201
Pembroke Pines, FL 33026
(954) 441-8881
http://www.f-cca.com/

The Florida-Caribbean Cruise Association is a trade group representing 12 member lines, operating almost

100 vessels in Florida, Caribbean, and Mexican waters. Created in 1972, the FCCA provides a forum for discussion on legislation, tourism development, port, safety, security, and other issues.

International Council of Cruise Lines
2111 Wilson Boulevard, 8th Floor
Arlington, VA 22201
(703) 522-8463
http://www.iccl.org/contact.cfm

The mission of the International Council of Cruise Lines (ICCL) is to participate in the regulatory and policy development process and promote all measures that foster a safe, secure and healthy cruise ship environment. ICCL's members include the largest passenger cruise lines that call on hundreds of ports in the United States and abroad. Each year ICCL's overnight cruise ship operators carry more than seven million passengers on over 90 ships. ICCL is dedicated to ensuring that the cruise industry provides a safe, healthy, secure, and caring shipboard environment for passengers and crew, minimizing the environmental impact of its vessel operations, and delivering a reliable, affordable, and enjoyable cruise experience.

GOLF COURSE SUPERINTENDENT

American Society of Golf Course Architects
125 N. Executive Drive, Suite 106
Brookfield, WI 53005
(262) 786-5960
info@asgca.org
http://www.golfdesign.org

The American Society of Golf Course Architects (ASGCA) was founded in 1946. Its members are actively involved with designing and building new golf courses or redesigning older courses. Members must have at least eight years of job experience. The ASGCA works to assure that golf course design is done in a manner that is environmentally responsible, and is involved with many issues related to the game and profession of golf. The ASGCA is a good source of information about golf course design, with examples of outstanding design and featured golf course architects.

Golf Course Superintendents Association of America
1421 Research Park Drive
Lawrence, KS 66049-3859
(785) 841-2240
infoxbox@gcsaa.org
http://www.gcsaa.org

The GCSAA, with more than 20,000 members, is the leading professional organization for men and women who manage golf courses in the United States and throughout the world. Members include superintendents, assistant superintendents, students, and educators. The association has 104 affiliated chapters, with members in more than 75 countries. The GCSAA offers certified programs that recognize high standards of professionalism achieved through education and experience. The association offers more than 200 annual seminars on such subjects as turf grass management, golf course construction, and business communication. It also offers scholarships to students planning careers in golf course management or turf grass science.

The Professional Golf Association of America
100 Avenue of the Champions
Palm Beach Gardens, FL 33418
(800) 618-5535
http://www.pga.com

The Professional Golf Association of America (PGA) was founded in 1916 and has grown into the world's largest sports organization. The PGA, which works to educate people about the game of golf and its benefits, has more than 28,000 members. Its Web site is huge, offering everything from TV golf schedules to tips on improving your game. There's also a section for junior golfers, notes on various types of golf equipment, statistics of professional players participating in the PGA tour, and much more.

United States Golf Association
PO Box 708
Far Hills, NJ 07931
(908) 234-2300
http://www.usga.org

The United States Golf Association was founded in 1894 to serve as the national governing body for golf. The nonprofit organization sponsors a variety of programs to enhance all levels of golf, and offers a members program for individuals who wish to support the sport of golf. The association is responsible for writing the rules and regulations that pertain to golf, and it sponsors 13 national championships each year. Its Web site provides reports on golf equipment, information about the rules of golf, and more.

HUMAN CANNONBALL

American Youth Circus Organization
PO Box 96
Temple, NH 03084
(603) 654-5523
info@americanyouthcircus.org
http://www.americanyouthcircus.org

AYCO promotes youth participation in circus arts. Its showcase event is the biennial international AYCO Festival. The festival includes workshops, discussion groups, performances by youth troupes from around North America, and special performances by circus stars of the future. AYCO also fosters communication among circus arts educators and organizations; provides circus arts coaches with training procedures and guidelines for safety standards; provides support for artistic performers wishing to pursue or expand their circus careers; promotes youth circus activities through public relations efforts and a biannual newsletter; and provides circus-related educational materials to schools and educators.

Circus Fans Association of America
2704 Marshall Avenue
Lorain, OH 44052
http://www.circusfans.org

The CFA was established in 1926 to enjoy and preserve the circus as an institution. This original goal is still the cornerstone of the organization. Members also monitor federal, state, and local legislation, and they sometimes find themselves involved case by case—testifying at hearings, passing out educational pamphlets, and keeping the public informed. The organization also produces a magazine six times a year.

The Circus Shop
http://www.circusshop.net/

The Web site offers a selection of circus equipment, books and videos, available primarily by mail order.

The Circus Space
Coronet Street
London N1 6HD
United Kingdom
+44 (0)20 7613 4141
http://www.thecircusspace.co.uk/

This registered charity specializes in the circus arts and is one of the top three circus schools in Europe. It is a member of the European Federation of Circus Schools and the United Kingdom's Circus Arts Forum. Circus Space offers a diverse artistic program that includes the only degree-level education in the circus arts in the United Kingdom, professional development opportunities for aspiring and established performers, participatory and leisure activities for young people and adults, and a varied performance program, including the annual Circus Space Festival. The group also provides affordable workspace for related arts companies and opportunities for private and public sector organizations to use circus skills as a staff development tool.

ICE RINK MANAGER

Rink Management Services
9400 Charter Crossing, Suite D
Mechanicsville, VA 23116
http://www.rinkmanagement.com/

Rink Management Services is the nation's largest manager of ice skating rinks, managing indoor and outdoor rinks; privately owned stand-alone rinks; privately owned mall rinks; and foundation and municipal rinks.

USA Hockey, Inc.
1775 Bob Johnson Drive
Colorado Springs, CO 80906
(719) 576-8724
http://www.usahockey.com

USA Hockey, Inc. is the national governing body for hockey in the United States. It promotes the growth of hockey by encouraging, developing, advancing, and administering the sport. USA Hockey is responsible for organizing and training U.S. men's and women's teams for international play. Its 585,000 members include ice and in-line hockey players, coaches, officials, and volunteers.

The organization's main emphasis is to support and develop grassroots programs. USA Hockey is divided into 11 districts, each of which has a registrar to register teams; a referee-in-chief to register officials and organize clinics; a coach-in-chief to administer educational programs for coaches; a risk manager to oversee liability and safety programs; and an initiation program administrator to set up learn-to-play programs. It publishes American Hockey Magazine for members.

U.S. Figure Skating
20 First Street
Colorado Springs, CO 80906
(719) 635-5200
http://www.usfigureskating.org/

U.S. Figure Skating is the official governing body for the sport of figure skating in the United States, recognized as such by both the United States Olympic Committee (USOC) and the International Skating Union (ISU). As the governing body, U.S. Figure Skating's mission is to provide programs to encourage participation and achievement in the sport of figure skating. Among other things, U.S. Figure Skating's status as governing body gives it the authority to regulate and govern the sport in the United States, create rules for the holding of tests, competitions, and other activities, and to organize and sponsor competitions for the purpose of stimulating interest in the sport.

Zamboni Merchandising Company, Inc.
PO Box 1248
Paramount, CA 90723
(562) 663-1650
info@zamboni.com
http://www.zamboni.com

The Zamboni Merchandising Company was founded in 1950 by inventor Frank J. Zamboni, the man who invented the original ice resurfacing machine. In 2001 *the company created the Frank J. Zamboni award to honor outstanding and innovative contributions to the ice skating industry. The company's Web site explains how the machines work and lists the different models available, has a special section for kids and students, and has lots of interesting facts about ice resurfacing and the machines used.*

IMAGE CONSULTANT

American Society for Training & Development
1640 King Street
Box 1443
Alexandria, VA 22313
(703) 683-8100
http://www.astd.org/ASTD/About_ASTD

American Society for Training & Development is the world's largest association dedicated to workplace learning and performance professionals. ASTD's 70,000 members and associates come from more than 100 countries and thousands of organizations—multinational corporations, medium-sized and small businesses, government, academia, consulting firms, and product and service suppliers. ASTD marks its beginning in 1944 when the organization held its first annual conference. In recent years, ASTD has widened the industry's focus to connect learning and performance to measurable results, and is a sought-after voice on critical public policy issues.

Association of Image Consultants International
431 East Locust Street, Suite 300
Des Moines, IA 50309
(515) 282-5500
info@aici.org
http://www.aici.org

A worldwide nonprofit professional association of men and women

specializing in visual appearance and verbal and nonverbal communication, who counsel both individual and corporate clients on appearance, behavior, and communication skills to help achieve their specific goals with authenticity, credibility, and confidence.

Federation of Image Consultants
http://www.tfic.org.uk

The professional body for the U.K.'s personal image industry. Its mission is to promote best practice in the industry, to set and develop standards for the image profession, and to promote the image industry in the UK and overseas.

International Association of Protocol Consultants
PO Box 6150
McLean VA 22106
(703) 759-4272

The IAPC provides executive education in leadership, international protocol, etiquette, and civility, and offers two certification programs for certified protocol consultant and certified protocol officer.

LIMOUSINE DRIVER

National Limousine Association
49 South Maple Avenue
Marlton, NJ 08053
(856) 596-3344
info@limo.org
http://www.limo.org

The National Limousine Association was founded in 1985 as a voluntary, nonprofit, tax-exempt organization dedicated to representing the worldwide, national, state, and local interests of the luxury chauffeured ground transportation industry. Members include limousine owners and operators, suppliers, manufacturers, and regional and state limousine associations. By pooling resources and knowledge of thousands of operators from around the world, the National Limousine Association hopes to accomplish goals that would be far beyond the scope of any single limousine company. Suppliers and manufacturers are welcome to join as associate members. NLA members work for overall improvement in the industry, partly by setting standards for professionalism.

National Association of Limousine Drivers and Chauffeurs

http://carscrvice.meetup.com/1

This Web site offers a nationwide chance for drivers to interact and exchange information about their job, and set up local meetings in their hometowns.

Taxicab, Limousine & Paratransit Association

3849 Farragut Avenue
Kensington, MD 20895
(301) 946-5701
http://www.tlpa.org/

Established in 1917, the Taxicab, Limousine & Paratransit Association (TLPA) is a nonprofit trade association of and for the private passenger transportation industry. The association's extensive membership includes 1,100 taxicab companies, executive sedan and limousine services, airport shuttle fleets, nonemergency medical transportation companies, and paratransit services. The association offers a network of programs, services, and support that will enhance members' ability to serve public transportation needs. The group is the leading information, education, and legislative resource in the passenger transportation industry.

It represents common federal legislative interests, protects industry rights and opportunities, provides industry information, and offers professional development and education.

MAGICIAN

Canadian Association of Magicians

http://www.canadianassociationof
magicians.com/HOMEPAGE.html

The Canadian Association of Magicians (CAM) is dedicated to the promotion and encouragement of magic and magicians in Canada. CAM magicians regularly compete at the European convention; the association publishes a magazine three times a year.

International Brotherhood of Magicians

http://www.magician.org/index.htm

The IBM is the world's largest organization for magicians, boasting nearly 15,000 members worldwide, with more than 300 local groups (called Rings) in more than 73 countries. Candidates for membership in the International Brotherhood of Magicians must have had a sincere interest in the art of magic for at least two years prior to application (one year for youth membership).

New England Magic Collectors Association

c/o Magic Art Studio
137 Spring Street
Watertown, MA 02472
http://www.nemca.com/

The New England Magic Collectors Association (NEMCA) was founded in 1980, drawing its membership from magic collectors and historians in the six New England states. NEMCA is a nonprofit organization devoted to collecting books, memorabilia, and apparatus related to magic and the allied arts, preserving the history and knowledge of magic, and sharing knowledge and expertise with other members.

Society of American Magicians
15 Warren Street
Hackensack, NJ 07601
Klownchuck@aol.com
http://www.magicsam.com

The Society of American Magicians offers the opportunity to associate with others in the world of magic, including professionals, amateurs, manufacturers, magic dealers, book authors, and magic collectors. Through its monthly publications, annual convention, and over 250 "assemblies" throughout the world, the society provides a forum for the advancement of magic through discussions, lectures, research, performances, and exchange of magic secrets. SAM presents awards and fellowships that recognize achievement in magic and awards scholarships for children, 10 to 18, to attend summer magic camp. The society seeks to advance and preserve magic as a performing art, promote fellowship in the world of magic, and maintain and improve ethical standards.

MINIATURE GOLF COURSE OWNER

Miniature Golf Association U.S.
1113 Belle Place
Fort Worth, TX 76107
(817) 738-5522
http://www.mgaus.org/

The Miniature Golf Association U.S. (MGAUS) is a trade association established in 1997 to open the lines of communication and to provide an effective forum for businesspeople interested in the continued growth and success of the miniature golf and family entertainment center industry. The MGAUS is dedicated to improving the safety and professionalism of miniature golf and family entertainment centers. The MGAUS agenda addresses the issues, opportunities, and problems which affect the miniature golf and family entertainment center industry. The MGAUS caters specifically to the needs, interests, and goals of its members by providing an information resource and communications network; market research and analysis; political lobbying; publications including The Right Track *newsletter,* The Miniature Golf Reference Manual & Buyers Guide, *and Action Alerts regarding important information; amusement industry management and employee training systems; a positive national and international image of the industry through the use of marketing; and problem resolution for members. The MGAUS Business Network of more than 5,000 contacts in the industry enables members to have almost immediate access to other operators, manufacturers, consultants, designers, builders, engineers, insurance companies, governmental agencies and officials, financial resources, expert witnesses, defense attorneys, training services, employment, and management services.*

Oasis Family Fun Park and Miniature Golf
97 North Greenbush Road
Troy, NY 12180
(518) 283-3646
http://www.oasispark.net/

This 19-hole miniature golf course is owned by Tom and Andrea Paone, along with a bumper boat pond and ice cream parlor. The Web site includes information about the park, details about birthday parties and tee shirts, and more.

Professional Miniature Golf Association

PO Box 7021
Appleton, WI 54913
(866) 713-7530
http://www.thepmga.com/

PMGA is an association of business professionals with a passion for miniature golf and an expertise in course planning and management. The association specializes in miniature golf business planning, promotional events, and the design and construction of miniature golf courses. With backgrounds in the fields of business development, financial planning, construction, and design, PMGA can help members maximize profits and materialize a vision. The association professionals help members solidify a marketing mix, return on investment, and cash flows to secure outside funding. Customized analysis includes traffic estimates, cost/revenue analysis, and cash flow. PMGA also can design custom miniature golf plans for themed courses, sport courses, and indoor courses.

U.S. ProMiniGolf Association

c/o Hawaiian Rumble
3210 Highway 17 S
North Myrtle Beach, SC 29582
(843) 458-2585
http://prominigolf.com

The U.S. ProMiniGolf Association is the sole recognized national affiliate representing the United States within the World Minigolf Sports Federation. The U.S. ProMiniGolf Association recognizes and sanctions the Masters National ProMiniGolf Championship held in Myrtle Beach, S.C., the fourth week of each September, as the official national championship forum whereby the top professional minigolfers in America come together in tournament play to decide who shall be the new national prominigolf champions. Six sanctioned prominigolf tournaments are held at the Masters National events that week.

PAINTBALL PARK OPERATOR

American Paintball Players Association

(612) 605-8323,
http://www.paintball-players.org/

Association Web site for paintball players, with information on players, teams, and pending paintball-related legislation.

National Collegiate Paintball Association

1133 Industrial Boulevard #6
Chippewa Falls, WI 54729
(715) 720-9131
ncpa@college-paintball.com
http://www.college-paintball.com

The NCPA is an all-volunteer, non-profit organization created by college players to promote paintball at the high school and college level. The NCPA and its member clubs organize recruitment drives, informational meetings, recreational club outings, charity events, intramural events and the national intercollegiate tournament league. NCPA also sanctions the annual College and High School Paintball National Championships. The association strives to present paintball to the public in a positive manner through its members' volunteer and legislative efforts. The NCPA also offers various benefits to members and awards an annual $500 college scholarship to a player who has good grades and promotes a positive image for paintball.

Paintball Magazine.net
http://www.paintballmagazine.net/
demisepb.html
A Web site with lots of information about paintball.

PARADE FLOAT DESIGNER

American Institute of Floral Designers
720 Light Street
Baltimore, MD 21230
(410) 752-3318
AIFD@assnhqtrs.com
http://www.aifd.org
The floral industry's leading nonprofit organization committed to establishing and maintaining higher standards in professional floral design. With over 1,200 members worldwide, AiFD and its members are in the forefront of the industry in presenting educational and design programs.

Phoenix Decorating Co.
835 South Raymond Avenue
Pasadena, CA 91105
(626) 793-3174
floats@phoenixdecoratingco.com
http://www.phoenixdecoratingco.com

Tournament of Roses
391 South Orange Grove Boulevard
Pasadena, CA 91184
(626) 449-4100
http://www.tournamentofroses.com
Web site home of the Tournament of Roses, which is held each New Year's Day in Pasadena, California, home of the Rose Parade and Rose Bowl Game. This celebration, more than a century old, is a festival of flowers, music, and sports, featuring all kinds of decorated floats.

PARTY PLANNER

Association of Catering and Event Professionals
PO Box 14223
Portland, OR 97293
(503) 299-2237
floralevent@aol.com
http://acep.com
The association aims to improve the status and represent the best interests of the catering and event planning industry. ACEP tries to promote among its members an exchange of ideas and solutions to industry problems. The association presents educational programs related to catering, party and event planning, and related businesses. ACEP offers an extensive list of businesses that provide services usually needed by caterers and party and event planners. The association holds 10 monthly meetings a year and invites speakers who address issues and problems in the catering and party and event planning industries. Meetings also offer opportunities for networking. The association annually awards a scholarship worth $750.

International Caterers Association
1200 17th Street NW
Washington, DC 20036
(888) 604-5844
http://www.icacater.org/home.php
The International Caterers Association is dedicated to the education of the catering industry, supporting, promoting, and improving all aspects of the catering business. The ICA produces publications, seminars, workshops, and demonstrations for trade and industry organizations throughout the year.

PERSONAL TRAINER

National Exercise and Sports Trainers Association
30245 Tomas
Rancho Santa Margarita, CA 92688
(877) 348-6692
http://www.nestacertified.com/

An association for personal training, sports conditioning, yoga, pilates, integrative fitness, and life coaching professionals. Since 1992, NESTA has been a leader in innovative solutions for fitness and wellness professionals and club owners. NESTA offers career training and business development options and provides complete solutions for health, fitness, and wellness professionals. The association's comprehensive educational programs combine science with practical, real-world experience to ensure that members have a well-rounded understanding of how to guide clients to their goals safely and effectively. NESTA offers business development systems for all types of individuals and companies who are in fields ranging from personal training to life coaching to yoga and pilates, and even massage therapy.

National Exercise Trainers Association
5955 Golden Valley Road, Suite 240
Minneapolis, MN 55422
(800) 237-6242
neta@netafit.org
http://www.ndeita.com

NETA is an education and training organization for fitness professionals. Since its founding in 1977, NETA has certified over 120,00 people and is recognized as a leader in the fitness industry. NETA offers certification and continuing education workshops in group exercise, personal training and Pilates. The association is a nonprofit organization aiming to provide the fitness industry with reasonably-priced education. In addition to education and training, NETA offers fitness professionals such products as music, videos, apparel, and other accessories. NETA hopes that by offering hands-on training and certification to all who are interested that it can help improve the quality of fitness instruction to the American public.

PRIVATE PARTY DISC JOCKEY

American Disc Jockey Association
20118 North 67th Avenue
Suite 300-605
Glendale, AZ 85308
(888) 723-5776
http://www.adja.org

An association of professional disc jockeys that provides continuous education, camaraderie, and networking to help each member act ethically and responsibly.

Canadian Disk Jockey Association
PO Box 92
Arva, Ontario N0M 1C0
Canada
(877) 472-0653 (toll free)
http://www.cdja.org/

The CDJA is a not-for-profit trade association of professional independent disc jockeys across Canada whose goal is to maintain a high standard and quality of performance, business ethics, and satisfaction for customers using professional disc jockeys for all wedding and party functions.

PROFESSIONAL SHOPPER

Gift Association of America
115 Rolling Hills Road
Johnstown, PA 15905-5225

(814) 288-1460
info@giftassn.com
http://www.giftassoc.org

GAA aspires to increase business efficiency by keeping members abreast of the newest methods of business operation through seminars, newsletters, and the GAA Web site. In addition, the GAA attempts to foster and preserve healthy, competitive conditions and unify the rapidly growing and widely varied gift industry. GAA strives to provide a comprehensive basic benefits package for members; train, educate, and assist members in improving their skills; encourage member involvement in GAA activities; and network with gift industry leaders to provide programs that will benefit GAA members worldwide.

International Virtual Assistants Association

561 Keystone Avenue, Suite 309
Reno, NV 89503
(888) 259-2487
http://www.ivaa.org

The International Virtual Assistants Association (IVAA) is a nonprofit organization dedicated to the professional education and development of members of the virtual assistance profession, and to educating the public on the role and function of the virtual assistant. A virtual assistant is an independent entrepreneur providing administrative, creative, and technical services. Using advanced technological modes of communication and data delivery, a professional VA assists clients in his/her area of expertise from his or her own office on a contractual basis. IVAA is the only organization offering the comprehensive IVAA Certified Virtual Assistant (CVA) exam, recognized internationally as the standard that virtual assistants strive to attain.

PSYCHIC

Association for Research and Enlightenment

215 67th Street
Virginia Beach, VA 23451
(800) 333-4499
http://www.edgarcayce.org

The Association for Research and Enlightenment, Inc. (ARE), is a not-for-profit organization founded in 1931 by Edgar Cayce, to research and explore transpersonal subjects such as holistic health, ancient mysteries, personal spirituality, dreams and dream interpretation, intuition, and philosophy and reincarnation. With an international headquarters in Virginia Beach, Virginia, the ARE community is a global network of individuals who offer conferences, educational activities, and fellowship around the world. More than 300 books have been written about Cayce's life and work, resulting in "Edgar Cayce Centers" in twenty-five countries, and members in more than 60 countries.

Parapsychological Association

2474-342 Walnut Street
Cary, NC 27511
http://www.parapsych.org/

The Parapsychological Association, Inc. (PA) is the international professional organization of scientists and scholars engaged in the study of 'psi' (or 'psychic') experiences, such as telepathy, clairvoyance, remote viewing, psychokinesis, psychic healing, and precognition. Such experiences seem to challenge contemporary conceptions of human nature and of the physical world, and appear to involve the transfer of information and the influence of physical systems independently of time and space, via mechanisms we cannot currently explain. The primary objective of the Parapsychological Association is to achieve a scientific understanding of these experiences. PA members develop and refine methodologies for studying psi and its physical, biological, or psychological underpinnings. They assess hypotheses and theories through experiments, conceptual models, and field investigations, and seek to integrate their findings with other scientific domains. PA members also explore the meaning and impact of psychic experiences in human society, and assess the possibility of practical applications and technologies.

GotPsi On-Line Psi Tests

http://www.gotpsi.com

A Web site that offers some informal tests for "psi" functioning based on the same techniques used in more formal laboratory experiments.

Victoria Laurie Web site

http://www.victorialaurie.com

Web site for Victoria Laurie, mystery author and psychic.

RENAISSANCE FESTIVAL PERFORMER

Association for Renaissance Martial Arts (Swords and Swordsmanship)

http://www.thearma.org/

The Association for Renaissance Martial Arts is an educational non-profit organization dedicated to the study and practice of historical fencing and the exploration and promotion of the Western martial heritage. The ARMA focuses on the interpretation and legitimate reconstruction of Medieval and Renaissance combat systems as a modern discipline. The ARMA teaches historical

fighting skills through a curriculum of reconstructed techniques, principles, and methods for using a variety of swords, spears, shields, staff weapons, daggers, and unarmed grappling and wrestling skills as taught in period books and manuscripts.

International Association of Fairs and Expos

3043 East Cairo
Springfield, MO 65802
(417) 862-5771
http://www.fairsandexpos.com

International Association of Fairs and Expositions (IAFE) is a voluntary, nonprofit corporation, organizing state, provincial, regional, and county agricultural fairs, shows, exhibitions, and expositions. Its associate members include state and provincial associations of fairs, nonagricultural expositions and festivals, associations, corporations, and individuals engaged in providing products and services to its members, all of whom are interested in the improvement of fairs, shows, expositions, and allied fields. The IAFE began in 1885 with a half dozen fairs. Today, the IAFE represents more than 1,300 fairs around the world, and more than 1,300 members from allied fields. Throughout the years, the IAFE has remained true to its purpose of promoting and encouraging the development and improvement of fairs, shows, and expositions.

International Wenches Guild

http://www.wench.org

The International Wenches Guild was founded at the New York Renaissance Faire in the summer of 1995. What began essentially as a local club intended to give some vague sense of order to wenches rapidly turned into an organization stretching across North

America, with a present membership of more than 2,000 women. Membership in the Guild is open to all interested parties, including men, and includes a pewter pin with the Guild logo on it, a "License to Wench," a membership card, The Little Brown Book, *and the* Official Guide.

Renaissance Magazine
One Controls Drive
Shelton, CT 06484
(800) 232-2224
http://www.renaissancemagazine.com
Magazine that includes all kinds of information about Renaissance faires.

Society for Creative Anachronism
PO Box 360789
Milpitas, CA 95036-0789
(408) 263-9305
directors@sca.org
http://www.sca.org
The SCA is dedicated to researching and re-creating the arts and skills of pre-17th-century Europe. The organization includes more than 30,000 members around the world. Members, dressed in clothing of the Middle Ages and Renaissance, attend tournaments, festivals, arts exhibits, classes, workshops, dancing, and feasts. The society's chapters are grouped in "kingdoms," which often cover more than one nation. SCA groups hold medieval forms of combat and practice chivalry and heraldry—the display of coats of arms. The society promotes inter-kingdom events and symposiums to promote education and research in its era of interest. SCA has its own "royalty," which holds courts at which members are recognized for their contributions. SCA through its Web site guides prospective members to the chapter nearest them and offers them advice on how to dress.

Wooden Weapons—Renaissance and Medieval Resources
http://www.woodenweapons.com/links.htm
Web site with all kinds of links to various resources listing weapons and other items useful for Renaissance Faire actors.

RINGMASTER

American Youth Circus Organization
PO Box 96
Temple, NH 03084
(603) 654-5523
info@americanyouthcircus.org
http://www.americanyouthcircus.org
AYCO promotes youth participation in circus arts. Its showcase event is the biennial international AYCO Festival. The festival includes workshops, discussion groups, performances by youth troupes from around North America, and special performances by circus stars of the future. AYCO also fosters communication among circus arts educators and organizations; provides circus arts coaches with training procedures and guidelines for safety standards; provides support for artistic performers wishing to pursue or expand their circus careers; promotes youth circus activities through public relations efforts and a biannual newsletter; and provides circus-related educational materials to schools and educators.

The Circus Shop
http://www.circusshop.net/
The Web site offers a selection of circus equipment, books, and videos, available primarily by mail order.

The Circus Space
Coronet Street
London N1 6HD
United Kingdom

+44 (0)20 7613 4141

http://www.thecircusspace.co.uk/

This registered charity specializes in the circus arts and is one of the top three circus schools in Europe. It is a member of the European Federation of Circus Schools and the United Kingdom's Circus Arts Forum. Circus Space offers a diverse artistic program that includes the only degree-level education in the circus arts in the United Kingdom, professional development opportunities for aspiring and established performers, participatory and leisure activities for young people and adults, and a varied performance program, including the annual Circus Space Festival. The group also provides affordable workspace for related arts companies and opportunities for private and public sector organizations to use circus skills as a staff development tool.

ROLLER COASTER DESIGNER

Amusement Industry Manufacturers and Suppliers International

1250 S.E. Port St. Lucie Boulevard

Suite C

Port St. Lucie, FL 34952

(772) 398-6701

http://www.aimsintl.org/

A nonprofit organization that represents amusement industry manufacturers and suppliers around the world. AIMS International does not manufacture or supply products, but is dedicated to continuing safety in the amusement industry. The association's purpose is to establish communications and foster working relations with other amusement industry trade associations and the government to promote and preserve the prosperity of the amusement industry.

Funderstanding Roller Coaster

http://www.funderstanding.com/k12/coaster

This simulator is designed for kids who want to design their own thrilling coaster and educators who want to use a cool activity to simulate the application of physics by using an exciting interactive tool and access to a wonderful reference source.

International Association of Amusement Parks and Attractions

1448 Duke Street

Alexandria, VA 22314

(703) 836-4800

convention@iaapa.org

http://www.iaapa.org

IAAPA was founded in 1918 and is a nonprofit organization with a membership including theme parks, family entertainment centers, zoos, aquariums, water parks, resorts, museums, and other amusement attractions as well as suppliers. IAAPA is dedicated to the preservation and prosperity of the amusement industry worldwide. It strives to promote safe operations and global development of companies and professional growth of employees. IAAPA has a code of ethics that asks members to provide wholesome and safe recreation, treat customers courteously, and conduct business with integrity. IAAPA is host each fall to a huge annual convention and trade show that displays the latest rides and other attractions for virtually any kind of amusement facility.

National Association of Amusement Ride Safety Officials

PO Box 638

Brandon, FL 33509-0638

(813) 661-2779

http://www.naarso.com/

The National Association of Amusement Ride Safety Officials is a nonprofit association of amusement ride inspectors representing jurisdictional agencies, insurance companies, private consultants, safety professionals, and federal government agencies.

Premier Rides
401 Headquarters Drive, Suite 201
Millersville, MD 21108
(410) 923-0414
info@premier-rides.com
http://www.premier-rides.com

One of the nation's leading roller coaster design companies, with an emphasis on innovation and ethical standards to help create maximum thrills while providing a commitment to guest safety, superior customer service, and quality and precision craftsmanship in all areas of ride design, fabrication, installation, and service.

RUNNING COACH

American Medical Athletic Association
4405 East-West Highway, Suite 405
Bethesda, MD 20814
(800) 776-2732
http://www.amaasportsmed.org/

Formerly the American Medical Joggers Association and now the professional division of the American Running Association, the AMAA is comprised of doctors and allied health care professionals who are committed to enhancing the well-being of patients through the promotion of running and exercise. The AMAA motivates physicians and other health care professionals to become active, and provides credible information on training, diet, injury prevention, and sports medicine to assist these professionals in motivating their patients to become active and lead healthy lifestyles. The association aims to provide medical and health professionals with information on the benefits of exercise and how to lead an active life, to develop motivational programs to encourage patients to lead active lifestyles, and to provide medical and health professionals with at least two quality continuing medical education events per year.

American Running Association
4405 East-West Highway, Suite 405
Bethesda, MD 20814
(800) 776-2732
http://www.americanrunning.org/

The American Running Association was founded in 1968 by Lt. Gen. Richard L. Bohannon, M.D., former Surgeon General of the U.S. Air Force and advocate for improving health through running. Originally called the National Jogging Association, the association changed its name in 1999 to the American Running Association (ARA). The association attempts to mobilize all Americans to use physical activity as a catalyst to deter and defeat youth obesity, to provide runners with information related to training, nutrition, sports medicine, and fitness; to develop motivational programs to encourage people to begin and maintain an active, healthy lifestyle; and to support runners by providing advice, motivational and educational programs, and referrals to sports-oriented professionals. Members include doctors, health professionals, teachers, coaches, CEOs, and others who believe in the importance of an active lifestyle.

Road Runners Club of America
8965 Guilford Road, Suite 150
Columbia, MD 21046
(410) 290-3890

office@rrca.org
http://www.rrca.org

The RRCA is a nonprofit organization that promotes long-distance running in the United States. It includes more than 670 running clubs and 160,000 members and maintains an extensive list of programs. They include providing sponsors and materials to dozens of clubs for low-key women's races across the country, holding workshops that promote safe running for women, and supporting running for the disabled. The RRCA offers a certification program that seeks to provide trained coaches for adult distance runners at all levels. It's hoped that certified coaches will help runners train intelligently, extend their running careers and minimize the risks of overuse injuries. The RRCA meets each spring for an annual meeting, workshops, awards banquet, and a national championship race.

SCI-FI CONVENTION PLANNER

Association of Destination Management Executives
3333 Quebec Street, Suite 4050
Denver, CO 80207
(937) 586-3727
http://www.adme.org

The Association of Destination Management Executives (ADME) is the only global nonprofit association dedicated to increasing the professionalism and effectiveness of destination management through education, promotion of ethical practices, and availability of information to the meetings, convention, and incentive travel industries, as well as the general public.

Convention Industry Council
8201 Greensboro Drive, Suite 300
McLean, VA 22102
http://www.conventionindustry.org

The Convention Industry Council's 30 member organizations represent more than 100,000 individuals, as well as 15,000 firms and properties involved in the meetings, conventions, and exhibitions industries. Formed in 1949 to provide a forum for member organizations seeking to enhance the industry, the CIC facilitates the exchange of information and develops programs to promote professionalism with the industry and educates the public on its profound economic impact. In addition to the CMP Program, CIC is also responsible for the Hall of Leaders Program as well as the Accepted Practices Exchange (APEX). APEX is working to unite the entire meeting, convention, and exhibition industry in the development and eventual implementation of voluntary standards.

International Special Events Society
401 North Michigan Avenue
Chicago, IL 60611
(312) 321-6853
http://www.ises.com

The International Special Events Society is comprised of more than 4,000 professionals in over a dozen countries representing special event producers (from festivals to trade shows), caterers, decorators, florists, destination management companies, rental companies, special effects experts, tent suppliers, audio-visual technicians, party and convention coordinators, balloon artists, educators, journalists, hotel sales managers, specialty entertainers, convention center managers, and many more.

Meeting Professionals International
4455 LBJ Freeway, Suite 1200
Dallas, TX 75244

(972) 702-3000
http://www.mpiweb.org

Established in 1972, Dallas-based Meeting Professionals International (MPI) is the largest association for the meetings profession with more than 20,000 members in 66 chapters and clubs. As the global authority and resource for the meetings and events industry, MPI empowers meeting professionals to increase their strategic value through education, clearly defined career pathways, and business growth opportunities.

The Professional Convention Management Association
2301 South Lake Shore Drive, Suite 1001
Chicago, IL 60616
(312) 423-7262
http://www.pcma.org

The Professional Convention Management Association (PCMA) is a nonprofit international association of professionals in the meetings industry whose mission is to deliver breakthrough education and promote the value of professional convention management.

Science Fiction and Fantasy Writers of America, Inc.
PO Box 877
Chestertown, MD 21620
execdir@sfwa.org
http://sfwa.org

SFWA was founded in 1965 by Damon Knight, who also served as its first president. The association has brought together many of the most successful science fiction writers throughout the world, and has grown in numbers and influence until it is now widely recognized as one of the most effective nonprofit writers' organizations in existence. Over 1,200 science fiction and fantasy writers, artists, editors, and allied professionals

are members. SFWA annually presents the Nebula Awards for the best science fiction or fantasy short story, novelette, novella, and novel of the year. SFWA protects the rights of writers by negotiating changes of language in publishers' contracts. It also represents members in grievances against publishers.

SKI LIFT OPERATOR

National Ski Areas Association
133 S. Van Gordon Street, Suite 300
Lakewood, CO 80228
(303) 987-1111
http://www.nsaa.org/nsaa/home/

The National Ski Areas Association is the trade association for ski area owners and operators, representing 326 alpine resorts that account for more than 90 percent of the skier/snowboarder visits nationwide. Its 400 supplier members provide equipment, goods, and services to the mountain resort industry. NSAA analyzes and distributes ski industry statistics; produces annual conferences and trade shows; produces a bimonthly industry publication, and is active in state and federal government affairs. The association also provides educational programs and employee training materials on industry issues including OSHA, ADA, and NEPA regulations and compliance; environmental laws and regulations; state regulatory requirements; aerial tramway safety; and resort operations and guest service.

Seasonal Human Resources Association
http://www.coolworks.com/shra/

Association of human resource and operations representatives from national park concessionaires, as well as resorts, cruise lines, ski areas, and more, who share a common interest in issues specific to seasonal employment, including recruiting, retention, staffing, training, housing, benefits, recreation, policies, and procedures. A conference is scheduled each fall, with the goal of continued education, legal updates, and networking.

Ski Tour Operators Association
PO Box 191981
Sacramento, CA 95819
http://www.skitops.com/news.htm

The Ski Tour Operators Association is an organization of the largest and best established ski tour operators in the United States and Canada. Founded in 1989, SkiTops has demanding criteria for membership to encourage professionalism and excellence. Many of the members have been in business for 20 years or longer and have strong repeat clientele.

United States Ski Association
PO Box 100
1500 Kearns Boulevard
Park City, UT 84060
(435) 649-9090
info@ussa.org
http://www.ussa.org

The association now also includes the U.S. Snowboard Association and is the national governing body for Olympic skiing and snowboarding. Founded in 1904, the organization provides leadership and direction for young skiers and snowboarders who seek to pursue the Olympic dream. USSA management and staff coordinate a nationwide program in seven Olympic sports—alpine, cross country, disabled, freestyle, ski jumping, Nordic combined, and snowboarding. USSA maintains an education and certification for coaches. The U.S. team has been based in Utah since 1974 and was consolidated with the ski and snowboard administration at Park City in 1988.

SKYDIVING INSTRUCTOR

British Parachute Association
5 Wharf Way
Glen Parva
Leicester LE2 9TF
United Kingdom
44 (0) 116 278 5271
http://www.bpa.org.uk/

The British Parachute Association was founded in 1962 to advance sport parachuting within the United Kingdom. The association's aim today is to encourage participation and promote excellence at all levels of skydiving from novice to world class competitor. Today there are about 35 affiliated parachute clubs throughout the United Kingdom and a membership of more than 30,000.

Canadian Sport Parachuting Association
300 Forced Road
Russell ON K4R 1A1
Canada
(613) 445-1881
http://www.cspa.ca/

The Canadian Sport Parachuting Association (CSPA), through affiliation with the Aero Club of Canada (ACC), is Canada's representative to the Federation Aeronautique Internationale (FAI), and is thereby the official sport organization for sport parachuting in Canada. Incorporated in 1956, CSPA promotes safe, enjoyable sport parachuting through cooperation and adherence to self-imposed rules and recommendations.

United States Parachute Association
1440 Duke Street
Alexandria, VA 22314
(703) 836-3495
membership@uspa.org
http://uspa.org

The USPA maintains an online directory of skydiving centers operated by its

*members. The association issues
four skydiving licenses, from A to D,
which indicate an individual's skill
and accomplishments. USPA certifies
instructors and establishes basic
safety and equipment standards for
member centers. The association offers
third-party liability insurance should
a member through skydiving cause
property damage and bodily injury.
USPA sanctions skydiving competitions
and documents national and world
records achieved by U.S. citizens. The
association selects the U.S. Parachute
team and conducts the National
Skydiving Championships. USPA also
publishes* Parachutist, *the nation's best-
known magazine for skydivers.*

STADIUM VENDOR

National Association of Concessionaires
35 East Wacker Drive, Suite 1816
Chicago, IL 60601
(312) 236-3858
info@NAConline.org
http://NAConline.org

*NAC is a trade association for the
recreation and leisure-time food and
beverage concessions industry. It
provides a highly diversified membership
with information and services aimed
at enhancing standards of quality
and professionalism throughout the
industry. NAC offers insurance policies
for members that cover such areas
as property, liability, and employee
benefits. The association holds an
annual convention, which features an
educational conference on a wide range
of topics and encourages interaction
among those in the concessions
industry. In conjunction with the annual
convention, NAC holds a trade show.
The association twice a year publishes a*

newsletter and a magazine, Concession
Profession.

Stadium Managers Association
525 SW 5th Street, Suite A
Des Moines, IA 50309
(515) 282-9117
http://www.stadiummanagers.org

*Formed in 1974, SMA promotes the
professional, efficient and state-of-the-
art management of stadiums around the
world. Its members are administrators
and operations personnel from teams,
government entities, colleges and
universities, and suppliers to the
industry.*

THEME PARK CHARACTER

**International Association of Amusement
Parks and Attractions**
1448 Duke Street
Alexandria, VA 22314
(703) 836-4800
convention@iaapa.org
http://www.iaapa.org

*IAAPA was founded in 1918 and is a
nonprofit organization with a membership
including theme parks, family
entertainment centers, zoos, aquariums,
water parks, resorts, museums, and
other amusement attractions as well
as suppliers. IAAPA is dedicated to
the preservation and prosperity of the
amusement industry worldwide. It
strives to promote safe operations and
global development of companies and
professional growth of employees. IAAPA
has a code of ethics that asks members to
provide wholesome and safe recreation,
treat customers courteously, and conduct
business with integrity. IAAPA is host
each fall to a huge annual convention and
trade show that displays the latest rides
and other attractions for virtually any
kind of amusement facility.*

THEME PARK MANAGER

Amusement Industry Manufacturers and Suppliers International
1250 S.E. Port St. Lucie Boulevard
Suite C
Port St. Lucie, FL 34952
(772) 398-6701
http://www.aimsintl.org/

A nonprofit organization that represents amusement industry manufacturers and suppliers around the world. AIMS International does not manufacture or supply products, but is dedicated to continuing safety in the amusement industry. The association's purpose is to establish communications and foster working relations with other amusement industry trade associations and the government to promote and preserve the prosperity of the amusement industry.

International Association of Amusement Parks and Attractions
1448 Duke Street
Alexandria, VA 22314
(703) 836-4800
convention@iaapa.org
http://www.iaapa.org

IAAPA was founded in 1918 and is a nonprofit organization with a membership including theme parks, family entertainment centers, zoos, aquariums, water parks, resorts, museums, and other amusement attractions as well as suppliers. IAAPA is dedicated to the preservation and prosperity of the amusement industry worldwide. It strives to promote safe operations and global development of companies and professional growth of employees. IAAPA has a code of ethics that asks members to provide wholesome and safe recreation, treat customers courteously, and conduct business with integrity. IAAPA is host each fall to a huge annual convention and trade show that displays the latest rides and other attractions for virtually any kind of amusement facility.

National Association of Amusement Ride Safety Officials
PO Box 638
Brandon, FL 33509
(800) 669-9053
http://www.naarso.com/

The National Association of Amusement Ride Safety Officials is a nonprofit association of amusement ride inspectors representing jurisdictional agencies, insurance companies, private consultants, safety professionals, and federal government agencies.

WINE CONSULTANT

American Society for Enology and Viticulture—Eastern Section
ASEV/ES Food Science Building
Purdue University
West Lafayette, IN 47907-1160
(765) 494-6704

This organization provides discussions on research and technology for the advancement of wines and solving problems of special interest to the enology and viticulture of grapes grown in the Eastern United States and Canada. The geographical area included in this organization includes all states east of the western borders of Minnesota, Iowa, Missouri, Arkansas, and Louisiana, plus the Canadian Provinces east of the Ontario-Manitoba border.

American Vineyard Foundation
Box 5779
Napa, CA 94581
(707) 252-6911
http://www.avf.org/

A California corporation organized in 1978 by the American Society of

Enology and Viticulture as a vehicle to raise funds for research in viticulture and enology.

California Association of Winegrape Growers
601 University Avenue, Suite 135
Sacramento, CA 85825
(800) 241-1800
info@cawg.org
http://www.cawg.org

CAWG represents the concerns of wine and concentrate grape growers. It strives to protect their interests and provide them with information and tools they need to remain competitive, well-informed and profitable. The association represents growers before legislative bodies, government agencies, and the news media. It provides an open forum to exchange ideas. It encourages cooperative efforts among grape growers to resolve issues related to growth and marketing. The association supports the production of quality wine grapes and works to stimulate their consumption. CAWG collects and distributes to members information on production and marketing. It helps present the annual United Wine and Grape Symposium, which combines seminars with a trade show.

Napa Valley Vintners Association
PO Box 141
St. Helena, CA 94574
(707) 963-3388
http://www.napavintners.com

Founded in 1943, the organization is a regional trade association with an active membership of 222 wineries, representing a tradition of dedicated vintners and grape growers who have worked and cared for this premier winegrowing region since the early 1800s.

Sonoma County Grape Growers Association
PO Box 1959
Sebastopol, CA 95473
(707) 829-3963
info@scgga.org
http://www.sonomagrapevine.org

The Sonoma County Grape Growers Association represents the farmers who grow grapes in Sonoma County. Grower members sell their grape production to wineries that make wine. Sonoma County grape growers take great pride in their land and the grapes they produce. Here the focus is on quality production because premium wines can only be made from high quality grapes.

APPENDIX B. ONLINE CAREER RESOURCES

This volume offers a look inside a wide range of unusual and unique careers that might appeal to someone interested in jobs in the leisure industry. And while it highlights general information, it's really only a glimpse into the jobs. The entries are intended to merely whet your appetite and provide you with some career options you may never have known existed.

Before jumping into any career, you'll want to do more research to make sure that it's really something you want to pursue. You'll most likely want to learn as much as you can about the careers in which you are interested. That way, as you continue to research and talk to people in those particular fields, you can ask informed and intelligent questions that will help you make your decisions. You might want to research the education options for learning the skills you'll need to be successful, along with scholarships, work-study programs, and other opportunities to help you finance that education. And, you might want answers to questions that weren't addressed in the information provided here. If you search long enough, you can find just about anything using the Internet, including additional information about the jobs featured in this book.

✳ **A word about Internet safety:** The Internet is also a wonderful resource for networking. Many job and career sites have forums where students can interact with other people interested in and working in that field. Some sites even offer online chats where people can communicate with each other in real time. They provide students and jobseekers opportunities to make connections and maybe even begin to lay the groundwork for future employment. But as you use these forums and chats, remember that anyone could be on the other side of that computer screen, telling you exactly what you want to hear. It's easy to get wrapped up in the excitement of the moment when you are on a forum or in a chat, interacting with people that share your career interests and aspirations. Be cautious about what kind of personal information you make available on the forums and in the chats; never give out your full name, address, or phone number. And never agree to meet with someone that you have met online.

SEARCH ENGINES

When looking for information, there are lots of search engines that will help you to find out more about these jobs along with others that might interest you. And while you might already have a favorite search engine, you might want to take some time to check out some of the others that are out there. Some have features that might help you find information not located with the others. Several engines will offer suggestions for ways to narrow your results, or related phrases you might want to search along with your search results. This is handy if you are having trouble locating exactly what you want.

Learn how to use the advanced search features of your favorite search engines. Knowing that might help you to zero in on exactly the information for which you are searching without wasting time looking through pages of irrelevant hits.

As you use the Internet to search information on the perfect career, keep in mind that like anything you find on the Internet, you need to consider the source from which the information comes.

Some of the most popular Internet search engines are:

AllSearchEngines.com
www.allsearchengines.com

This search engine index has links to the major search engines along with search engines grouped by topic. The site includes a page with more than 75 career and job search engines at http://www. allsearchengines.com/careerjobs.html.

AlltheWeb
http://www.alltheweb.com

AltaVista
http://www.altavista.com

Ask.com
http://www.ask.com

Dogpile
http://www.dogpile.com

Excite
http://www.excite.com

Google
http://www.google.com

HotBot
http://www.hotbot.com

LookSmart
http://www.looksmart.com

Lycos
http://www.lycos.com

Mamma.com
http://www.mamma.com

MSN Network
http://www.msn.com

My Way
http://www.goto.com

Teoma
http://www.directhit.com

Vivisimo
http://www.vivisimo.com

Yahoo!
http://www.yahoo.com

HELPFUL WEB SITES

The Internet is a wealth of information on careers—everything from the mundane to the outrageous. There are thousands of sites devoted to helping you find the perfect job for your interests, skills, and talents. The sites listed here are some of the most helpful ones that the authors came across and/or used while researching the jobs in this volume. The sites are listed in alphabetical order. They are offered for your information and are not endorsed by the authors.

All Experts
http://www.allexperts.com

"The oldest and largest free Q&A service on the Internet," AllExperts.com has thousands of volunteer experts to answer your questions. You can also read replies to questions asked by other people. Each expert has an online profile to help you pick someone who might be best suited to answer your question. Very easy to use, it's a great resource for finding experts who can help to answer your questions.

America's Career InfoNet
http://www.acinet.org

A wealth of information! You can get a feel for the general job market; check out wages and trends in a particular state for different jobs; and learn more about the knowledge, skills, abilities, and tasks for specific careers; and learn about required certifications and how to get them. You can search over 5,000 scholarship and other financial opportunities to help you further your education. A huge career resources library has links to nearly 6,500 online resources. And for fun, you can take a break and watch one of nearly 450 videos featuring real people at work; everything from custom tailors to engravers, glassblowers to silversmiths.

Backdoor Jobs: Short-Term Job Adventures, Summer Jobs, Volunteer Vacations, Work Abroad and More
http://www.backdoorjobs.com

This is the Web site of the popular book by the same name, now in its third edition. While not as extensive as the book, the site still offers a wealth of information for people looking for short-term opportunities: internships, seasonal jobs, volunteer vacations, and work abroad situations. Job opportunities are classified into several categories: Adventure Jobs, Camps, Ranches & Resort Jobs, Ski Resort Jobs, Jobs in the Great Outdoors, Nature Lover Jobs, Sustainable Living and Farming Work, Artistic & Learning Adventures, Heart Work, and Opportunities Abroad.

Boston Works—Job Explainer
http://bostonworks.boston.com/globe/job_explainer/archive.html

For nearly 18 months, the Boston Globe *ran a weekly series profiling a wide range of careers. Some of the jobs were more traditional, but with a twist, such as the veterinarian who makes house calls. Others were very unique and unusual, like the profile of a Superior of Society monk. The profiles discuss an "average" day, challenges of the job, required training, salary, and more. Each profile gives an up-close, personal look at that particular career. In addition, The Boston Works Web site (http://bostonworks.boston.com) has a lot of good, general employment-related information.*

Career Guide to Industries
http://www.bls.gov/oco/cg/cgindex.htm

For someone interested in working in a specific industry, but maybe undecided about exactly what career to pursue, this site is the place to start. Put together by the U.S. Department of Labor, you can learn more about the industry, working conditions, employment, occupations (in the industry), training and advancement, earnings, outlook, and sources of additional information.

Career Planning at About.com
http://careerplanning.about.com

Like most of the other About.com topics, the career planning area is a wealth of information, and links to other information on the Web. Among the excellent essentials are career planning A-to-Z, a career planning glossary, information on career choices, and a free career planning class. There are many great articles and other excellent resources.

Career Prospects in Virginia
http://www3.ccps.virginia.edu/career_prospects/default-search.html

Career Prospects is a database of entries with information about over 400 careers. Developed by the Virginia Career Resource Network, the online career information resource of the Virginia Department of Education, Office of

Career and Technical Education Services, the site was intended as a source of information about jobs "important to Virginia" but it's actually a great source of information for anyone. While some of the information like wages, outlook, and some of the requirements may apply only to Virginia, the other information for each job, like what's it like, getting ahead, skills, and the links will be of help to anyone interested in that career.

Career Voyages
http://www.careervoyages.gov

"The ultimate road trip to career success," sponsored by the U.S. Department of Labor and the U.S. Department of Education. This site features sections for students, parents, career changers, and career advisors with information and resources aimed to that specific group. The FAQ offers great information about getting started, the high-growth industries, how to find your perfect job, how to make sure you're qualified for the job you want, tips for paying for the training and education you need, and more. Also interesting are the hot careers and emerging fields sections.

Cruise Ship Employment
http://www.shipjobs.com/

An amazing collection of job and career resources for the cruise ship industry. You can find everything from links to careers to information about researching companies and employers. This is a great place to find just about anything you might be looking for, and probably lots of things you aren't looking for— everything from what are your chances of landing a job, terrorism and cruise jobs, how to waste your time looking for a cruise job, what is a crewing agency, and lots of stories.

Dream Jobs
http://www.salary.com/careers/
layouthtmls/crel_display_Cat10.html

The staff at Salary.com takes a look at some wild, wacky, outrageous, and totally cool ways to earn a living. The jobs they highlight include pro skateboarder, computer game guru, nose, diplomat, and much more. The profiles don't offer links or resources for more information, but they are informative and fun to read.

Find It! in DOL
http://www.dol.gov/dol/findit.htm

A handy source for finding information at the extensive U.S. Department of Labor Web site. You can Find It! by broad topic category, or by audience, which includes a section for students.

Fine Living: *Radical Sabbatical*
http://www.fineliving.com/fine/radical_
sabbatical

The show Radical Sabbatical *on the Fine Living network looks at people willing to take a chance and follow their dreams and passions. The show focuses on individuals between the ages of 20 and 65 who have made the decision to leave successful, lucrative careers to start over, usually in an unconventional career. You can read all about these people and their journeys on the show's Web site.*

Free Salary Survey Reports and Cost-of-Living Reports
http://www.salaryexpert.com

Based on information from a number of sources, Salary Expert will tell you what kind of salary you can expect to make for a certain job in a certain geographic location. Salary Expert has information on hundreds of jobs; everything from your more traditional white- and blue-collar jobs, to some unique and

out of the ordinary professions like
acupressurist, blacksmith, denture
waxer, taxidermist, and many others.
With sections covering schools, crime,
community comparison, community
explorer, and more, the moving center
is a useful area for people who need to
relocate for training or employment.

Fun Jobs

http://www.funjobs.com

*Fun Jobs has job listings for adventure,
outdoor, and fun jobs at ranches, camps,
ski resorts, and more. The job postings
have a lot of information about the
position, requirements, benefits, and
responsibilities so that you know what you
are getting into ahead of time. And, you
can apply online for most of the positions.
The* Fun Companies *link will let you look
up companies in an A-to-Z listing, or you
can search for companies in a specific
area or by keyword. The company listings
offer you more detailed information
about the location, types of jobs available,
employment qualifications, and more.*

Girls Can Do

http://www.girlscando.com

*"Helping Girls Discover Their
Life's Passions," Girls Can Do has
opportunities, resources, and a lot of
other cool stuff for girls ages 8 to 18.
Girls can explore sections on* Outdoor
Adventure, Sports, My Body, The Arts,
Sci-Tech, Change the World, *and* Learn,
Earn, and Intern. *In addition to reading
about women in all sorts of careers, girls
can explore a wide range of opportunities
and information that will help them grow
into strong, intelligent, capable women.*

Great Web Sites for Kids

http://www.ala.org/gwstemplate.cfm?se
ction=greatwebsites&template=/cfapps/
gws/default.cfm

*Great Web Sites for Kids is a collection
of more than 700 sites organized into a
variety of categories, including animals,
sciences, the arts, reference, social sciences,
and more. All of the sites included here
have been approved by a committee made
up of professional librarians and educators.
You can even submit your favorite site for
possible inclusion.*

Hospitality Jobs Online

http://www.hospitalityonline.com/

*Hospitality Jobs Online features
worldwide resort jobs with ski and
snowboard resorts, camps, national
parks, cruise ships, restaurants, and
hotels. The site includes a newsletter, job
profiles, articles and advice, and all sorts
of job ads.*

Hot Jobs—Career Tools Home

http://www.hotjobs.com/htdocs/tools/
index-us.html

*While the jobs listed at Hot Jobs are
more on the traditional side, the* Career
Tools *area has a lot of great resources
for anyone looking for a job. You'll find
information about how to write a resume
and a cover letter, how to put together a
career portfolio, interviewing tips, links
to career assessments, and much more.*

Job Descriptions & Job Details

http://www.job-descriptions.org

*Search for descriptions and details for more
than 13,000 jobs at this site. You can search
for jobs by category or by industry. You'd
probably be hard pressed to find a job that
isn't listed here, and you'll probably find
lots of jobs you never imagined existed. The
descriptions and details are short, but it's
interesting and fun, and might lead you to
the career of your dreams.*

Job Hunter's Bible

http://www.jobhuntersbible.com

This site is the official online supplement to the book What Color Is Your Parachute? A Practical Manual for Job-Hunters and Career-Changers, *and is a great source of information with lots of informative, helpful articles and links to many more resources.*

Job Profiles
http://www.jobprofiles.org

A collection of profiles where experienced workers share about the rewards of their job; stressful parts of the job; basic skills the job demands; challenges of the future; and advice on entering the field. The careers include everything from baseball ticket manager to pastry chef and much, much more. The hundreds of profiles are arranged by broad category. While most of the profiles are easy to read, you can check out the How to browse JobProfile. org *section (http://www.jobprofiles.org/ jphowto.htm) if you have any problems.*

Major Job Web Sites at Careers.org
http://www.careers.org/topic/01_jobs_ 10.html

This page at the careers.org Web site has links for more than 40 of the Web's major job-related Web sites. While you're there, check out the numerous links to additional information.

Monster Jobs
http://www.monster.com

Monster.com is one of the largest, and probably best known, job resource sites on the Web. It's really one-stop shopping for almost anything job-related that you can imagine. You can find a new job, network, update your resume, improve your skills, plan a job change or relocation, and so much more. Of special interest are the Monster: Cool Careers (http://change. monster.com/archives/coolcareers) and the Monster: Job Profiles (http://jobprofiles.

monster.com) where you can read about some really neat careers. The short profiles also include links to additional information. The Monster: Career Advice section (http://content.monster.com/) has resume and interviewing advice, message boards where you can network, relocation tools and advice, and more.

Occupational Outlook Handbook
http://www.bls.gov/oco

Published by the U.S. Department of Labor's Bureau of Labor Statistics, the Occupational Outlook Handbook *(sometimes referred to as the OOH) is the premiere source of career information. The book is updated every two years, so you can be assured that the information you are using to help make your decisions is current. The online version is very easy to use; you can search for a specific occupation, browse though a group of related occupations, or look through an alphabetical listing of all the jobs included in the volume. Each of the entries will highlight the general nature of the job, working conditions, training and other qualifications, job outlook, average earning, related occupations, and sources of additional information. Each entry covers several pages and is a terrific source to get some great information about a huge variety of jobs.*

ResortJobs.com
http://www.resortjobs.com/

ResortJobs.com features worldwide resort jobs with ski and snowboard resorts, camps, national parks, cruise ships, restaurants, and hotels. The site includes a newsletter, job profiles, articles and advice, and all sorts of job ads.

The Riley Guide: Employment Opportunities and Job Resources on the Internet
http://www.rileyguide.com

The Riley Guide is an amazing collection of job and career resources. Unless you are looking for something specific, one of the best ways to maneuver around the site is with the A-to-Z Index. You can find everything from links to careers in enology to information about researching companies and employers. The Riley Guide is a great place to find just about anything you might be looking for, and probably lots of things you aren't looking for. But, be forewarned, it's easy to get lost in the A-to-Z Index, reading about all sorts of interesting things.

USA TODAY Career Focus

http://www.usatoday.com/careers/dream/dreamarc.htm

Several years ago, USA TODAY ran a series featuring people working in their dream jobs. In the profiles, people discuss how they got their dream job, what they enjoy the most about it, they talk about an average day, their education backgrounds, sacrifices they had to make for their jobs, and more. They also share words of advice for anyone hoping to follow in their footsteps. Most of the articles also feature links where you can find more information. The USATODAY.com Job Center (http://www.usatoday.com/money/jobcenter/front.htm) also has links to lots of resources and additional information.

CAREER TESTS AND INVENTORIES

If you have no idea what career is right for you, there are many resources available online that will help assess your interests and maybe steer you in the right direction.

While some of the assessments charge a fee, there are many out there that are free. You can locate more tests and inventories on the Internet by doing a search for "career tests," "career inventories," or "personality inventories." Some of the most popular assessments available online are:

Campbell Interest and Skill Survey (CISS)
http://www.usnews.com/usnews/edu/careers/ccciss.htm

Career Explorer
http://careerexplorer.net/aptitude.asp

Career Focus 2000 Interest Inventory
http://www.iccweb.com/careerfocus

The Career Interests Game
http://career.missouri.edu/students/explore/thecareerinterestsgame.php

The Career Key
http://www.careerkey.org

CAREERLINK Inventory
http://www.mpc.edu/cl/cl.htm

Career Maze
http://www.careermaze.com/home.asp?licensee=CareerMaze

Career Tests at CareerPlanner.com
http://www.careerplanner.com

FOCUS
http://www.focuscareer.com

Keirsey Temperament Test
http://www.keirsey.com

Motivational Appraisal of Personal Potential (MAPP)
http://www.assessment.com

Myers-Briggs Personality Type
http://www.personalitypathways.com/type_inventory.html

Princeton Review Career Quiz
http://www.princetonreview.com/cte/
quiz/default.asp

Skills Profiler
http://www.acinet.org/acinet/skills_home.
asp

READ MORE ABOUT IT

AERIALIST

Heller, Carrie. *Aerial Training and Safety Manual.* Parker, Col.: National Writers Press, 2004.

Schreiber, Mark. *Dreams of the Solo Trapeze: Offstage with the Cirque de Soleil.* Columbus, Ohio: Canal House, 2004.

Sugarman, Robert. *Circus for Everyone: Circus Learning Around the World.* Shaftsbury, Vt.: Mountainside Press, 2001.

AUCTIONEER

Klemperer, Paul. *Auctions: Theory and Practice.* Princeton, N.J.: Princeton University Press, 2004.

Kuiper, Koenraad. *Smooth Talkers: The Linguistic Performance of Auctioneers and Sportscasters.* Mahwah, N.J.: Lawrence Erlbaum, 1996.

CASINO DEALER

International Gaming Institute. *The Gaming Industry: Introduction and Perspectives.* New York: John Wiley, 1996.

Paymar, Dan. *The Professional Poker Dealer's Handbook.* Henderson, Nev.: Two Plus Two Publishers, 1998.

CLUB MED HOST

Hart, Christopher. *Club Med.* Boston: Harvard Business School, 1990.

Rossin-Arthiat, Andre S. *Working for Club Med.* Quebec: Auslander Publishing, 1998.

CONVENTION PLANNER

Allen, Judy. *Event Planning: The Ultimate Guide to Successful Meetings, Corporate Events, Fundraising Galas, Conferences, Conventions, Incentives and Other Special Events.* New York: John Wiley, 2000.

Boehme, Ann J. *Planning Successful Meetings and Events: A Take-Charge Assistant Book.* New York: AMACOM, 1998.

CORPORATE CONCIERGE

Giovanni, K.C., and Ron Giovanni. *The Concierge Manual.* Apex, N.C.: New Road Publishing, 2002.

Stiel, Holly, and Delta Collins. *Ultimate Service: The Complete Handbook to the World of the Concierge.* Englewood Cliffs, N.J.: Prentice Hall, 1994.

CRUISE SHIP ACTIVITY DIRECTOR

Bow, Sandra. *Working on Cruise Ships.* San Francisco: Vacation Work Publications, 2002.

Kennedy, Don. *How To Get A Job On A Cruise Ship.* New York: Careersource Publications, 2000.

GOLF COURSE SUPERINTENDENT

Milligan, Robert A., and Thomas R. Maloney. *Human Resource Management for Golf Course Superintendents.* Hoboken, N.J.: John Wiley & Sons, 1996.

Quast, Danny H. *Golf Course Management: Tolls and Techniques*. New York: McGraw-Hill Professional, 2003.

HUMAN CANNONBALL

Davis, Janet M. *The Circus Age: Culture and Society under the American Big Top*. Chapel Hill, N.C.: University of North Carolina Press, 2002.

Feller, Bruce. *Under the Big Top: A Season with the Circus*. New York: Perennial, 2003.

ICE RINK MANAGER

Campbell, Kit, and John Geraint. *Handbook of Sports and Recreational Building Design, Volume 3*. Princeton, N.J.: Architectural Press, 1996.

Shulman, Carole. *The Complete Book of Figure Skating*. Champaign, Ill.: Human Kinetics, 2001.

IMAGE CONSULTANT

Goulet, Tag, and Rachel Gurevich. *FabJob Guide to Become an Image Consultant*. Seattle: FabJob.com, Inc., 2005.

Farr, Kendall. *The Pocket Stylist: Behind-the-Scenes Expertise from a Fashion Pro on Creating Your Own Look*. New York: Gotham, 2004.

LIMOUSINE DRIVER

Goerl, William J. *Wheels of Gold: A Complete How-To Guide for Starting a Million Dollar Limousine Business*. Paradise, Calif.: Paradise Planning, Inc., 2003.

Holly, Lou. *How to Succeed in the Limousine Business*. Chicago: All Charter Publications, 2001.

MAGICIAN

Boyar, Jay. *Be a Magician!: How to Put on a Magic Show and Mystify Your Friends*. New York: Julian Messner, 1981.

Goldberg, Jan. *Careers for Class Clowns & Other Engaging Types*. New York: McGraw-Hill, 2005.

Johnson, Karl. *The Magician and the Card Sharp: The Search for America's Greatest Sleight-of-Hand Artist*. New York: Henry Holt and Co., 2005.

Steinmeyer, Jim. *Hiding the Elephant: How Magicians Invented the Impossible and Learned to Disappear*. New York: Carroll & Graf Publishers, 2003.

MINIATURE GOLF COURSE OWNER

Mintzer, Richard, and Peter Grossman. *The Everything Golf Mini Book*. Boston: Adams Media Corporation, 2001.

PAINTBALL PARK OPERATOR

Cooper, Jeff. *Art of The Rifle*. Boulder, Colo.: Paladin Press, 1997.

Hanenkrat, Frank T. *The New Position Rifle Shooting: A How-To Text For Shooters and Coaches*. Oak Harbor, Ohio: Target Sports Education Center, 1997.

PARADE FLOAT DESIGNER

Schindler, Henri. *Mardi Gras Treasures: Float Designs of the Golden Age*. New York: Pelican Publishing Company, 2001.

PARTY PLANNER

Singleton, Suzanne. *Clever Party Planning*. Sparks, Md.: Twenty-Nine Angels Publishing, 1999.

Warner, Diane. *Diane Warner's Big Book of Parties: Creative Party Planning for Every Occasion.* Syracuse, N.Y.: New Page Books, 1999.

PERSONAL TRAINER

O'Brien, Teri S. *The Personal Trainer's Handbook.* Champaign, Ill.: Human Kinetics Publishers, 2003.

St. Michael, Melyssa and Linda Formichelli. *Becoming a Personal Trainer for Dummies.* New York: For Dummies/Wiley, 2004.

PRIVATE PARTY DISC JOCKEY

Broughton, Frank, and Bill Brewster. *How to DJ Right: The Art and Science of Playing Records.* New York: Grove Press, 2003.

Fresh, Chuck. *How To Be A DJ: Your Guide to Becoming a Radio, Nightclub or Private Party DJ.* Boston: Modern Rock Entertainment, 2001.

PROFESSIONAL SHOPPER

Lumpkin, Emily S. *Get Paid to Shop: Be a Personal Shopper for Corporate America.* Columbia, S.C.: Forte Publishing, 1999.

McBride, Laura Harrison, Peter J. Gallanis, and Tag Goulet. *FabJob Guide to Become a Personal Shopper.* Seattle: Fabjob.com, 2003.

PSYCHIC

Day, Laura. *Practical Intuition.* New York: Broadway, 1997.

———. *The Circle.* New York: Tarcher, 2001.

Laurie, Victoria. *Abby Cooper, Psychic Eye.* New York: Signet, 2004.

———. *Better Read than Dead: A Psychic Eye Mystery.* New York: Signet, 2005.

———. *A Vision of Murder: A Psychic Eye Mystery.* New York: Signet, 2005.

RENAISSANCE FESTIVAL PERFORMER

Strong, Roy. *Art and Power: Renaissance Festivals 1450-1650.* Berkeley, Calif.: University of California Press, 1985.

RINGMASTER

Antekeir, Kristopher. *Ringmaster! My Year on the Road With "The Greatest Show on Earth."* New York: E.P. Dutton, 1989.

Hammerstrom, David Lewis. *Big Top Boss: John Ringling North and the Circus.* Champaign, Ill.: University of Illinois Press, 1994.

ROLLER COASTER DESIGNER

Schutzmannsky, Klaus. *Roller Coaster: The Roller Coaster Designer Werner Stengel.* New York: Kehrer Verlag, 2003.

Urbanowicz, Steven J. *The Roller Coaster Lover's Companion: A Thrill Seeker's Guide to the World's Best Coasters.* New York: Citadel Press, 2002.

RUNNING COACH

Burfoot, Amby. *Runner's World Complete Book of Running.* Emmaus, Pa.: Rodale Books, 1999.

Fixx, James. *The Complete Book of Running.* New York: Random House, 1977.

SCI-FI CONVENTION PLANNER

DeCandidos, Keith R.A. *Articles of the Federation (Star Trek)*. New York: Simon & Schuster, 2005.

Svehla, Gary J. and Susan. *Fantastic Journeys: Sci-Fi Memories*. Baltimore, Md.: Luminary Press, 2003.

SKI LIFT OPERATOR

McKinnon, N.D. *Lift operator's handbook*. Iowa City, Iowa: NDM Services, 1976.

Pybus, Victoria. *Working in Ski Resorts —Europe and North America*. Oxford, England: Vacation Works Publications, 2003.

SKYDIVING INSTRUCTOR

Buchanan, Tom. *JUMP!: Skydiving Made Fun & Easy*. New York: McGraw-Hill Professional, 2003.

Poynter, Dan, and Mike Turoff. *Parachuting: The Skydiver's Handbook*. Santa Barbara, Calif.: Para Publishing, 2003.

STADIUM VENDOR

Smith, Curt. *Storied Stadiums: Baseball's History Through Its Ballparks*. New York: Carroll & Graf Publishers, 2001.

Solveig Paulson, Russell. *Peanuts, Popcorn, Ice Cream, Candy and Soda Pop and How They Began*. Nashville, Tenn.: Abingdon Press, 1970.

THEME PARK CHARACTER

Grant, John. *Encyclopedia of Walt Disney's Animated Characters: From Mickey Mouse to Hercules*. Burbank, Calif.: Disney Editions, 1998.

THEME PARK MANAGER

Baine, Celeste. *The Fantastical Engineer: A Thrillseeker's Guide to Careers in Theme Park Engineering*. Eugene, Ore.: Bonamy Publishing, 2000.

Birnbaum. *Birnbaum's Walt Disney World 2005: Expert Advice from the Inside Source*. Tampa, Fla.: Disney Editions, 2004.

WINE CONSULTANT

MacNeil, Karen. *The Wine Bible*. New York: Workman Publishing Company, 2001.

McCarthy, Ed. *Wine for Dummies*. New York: For Dummies/Wiley, 2003.

INDEX